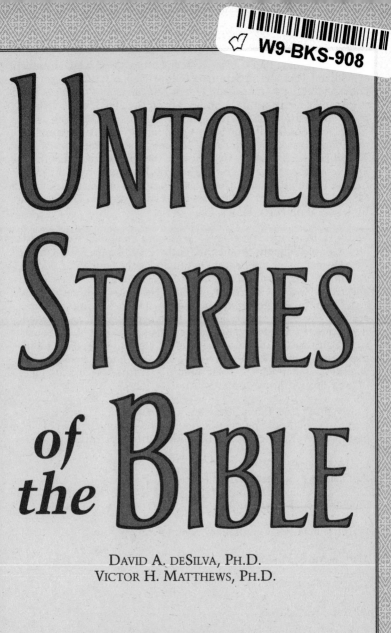

UNTOLD STORIES of the BIBLE

DAVID A. deSILVA, PH.D.
VICTOR H. MATTHEWS, PH.D.

PUBLICATIONS INTERNATIONAL, LTD.

David A. deSilva, Ph.D., is an associate professor of New Testament at Ashland Theological Seminary (Ohio). He has written several books including *4 Maccabees, Honor Discourse and the New Testament*, and a forthcoming commentary on the Epistle to the Hebrews. In addition, he has published numerous articles such as "The Dead Sea Scrolls and Early Christianity" and contributed to the *Dictionary of the Later New Testament* and *Dictionary of New Testament Backgrounds*. He serves on the editorial board of the *Journal for the Study of New Testament*. He contributed the following to this publication: Introduction; Part I: Abraham, Jacob, Joseph, Moses, Prophets; Part II: Maccabean Revolt, Egyptian Judaism; Part III: Jesus' Trial, Peter, James, Paul.

Victor H. Matthews, Ph.D. in Near Eastern and Judaic Studies, is a professor of Religious Studies at Southwest Missouri State University. His extensive publication list includes the books *The Old Testament: Text and Context* and *Old Testament Parallels: Stories and Laws from the Ancient Near East*. He contributed numerous articles to the *Anchor Bible Dictionary*, and his writing often appears in *The Bible Today, Biblical Theology Bulletin*, and *Biblical Archaeologist*. Dr. Matthews has served as president of the Southwest Commission on Religious Studies. He contributed the following to this publication: Part I: Adam and Eve, Enoch, Noah, Judges, Solomon, Esther; Part II: Tobit, Judith; Part III: Mary and Joseph, Infancy Stories, Jesus' Ministry, Andrew, John.

Contents

❖ ❖ ❖ ❖

Introduction • 6

Part I: Stories from the Hebrew Scriptures

Introduction

❖ ❖ ❖ ❖

D ID YOU EVER wonder about the life of Adam and Eve after they were thrown out of Eden, or why God should select Abraham of all people to become the founder of a chosen race, or about Moses' life in the court of Pharaoh after he was pulled out of the river? Did you ever think about what Jesus must have been like as a child, or what his father thought about him in later life, or what became of apostles like Peter, John, and Paul? If you have, you are not alone. Many Jews and Christians, knowing what the Bible does say about these figures, have longed to know more than biblical pages reveal. Over the centuries, a multitude of legends developed to fill in gaps in the Bible's stories. Some explain troubling details in the Bible, while others use a biblical story as a launching point for a new revelation or moral exhortation. Still others simply provide more information about those interesting figures about whom people wished the Bible said more.

This book will introduce you to many stories about figures from the Bible—some whose names will be familiar and others who will be unfamiliar. These stories were told during the last three centuries before and first two centuries after the turn of the era (300 B.C.–A.D. 200). These stories are not presented here as "true" in the sense of preserving accurate information about historical events. It is unlikely that any of the non-biblical

Opposite: *Various extrabiblical sources discuss the childhood of Jesus. He is shown in this depiction with his father, Joseph.*

stories presented here (with the exception of the Maccabean Revolt in Part II) actually happened. The stories do tell us something valuable, however, about the way in which early Jews read their Scriptures, dealt with perceived problems in the biblical stories, derived and passed on moral instruction, and enhanced their sense of identity in the midst

After King Antiochus tries to destroy the Jewish way of life, Judas Maccabaeus leads a successful revolt.

of a world dominated by non-Jews. Some stories about Old Testament (Hebrew Bible) personalities were preserved by Christian authors, giving us insight into the importance of figures like Isaiah and Jeremiah in the early church. Traditions and legends about Jesus, and the activities of his inner circle of apostles also tell us something about the interest of the early church in its founders. Thus the ways in which the Bible was expanded and rewritten will certainly provide a window into the past, but not the distant past of Abraham, Moses, or even Jesus. Rather, it will open a window for us into the piety and concerns of the extrabiblical writers and their audience.

Part I gathers together material from outside the Bible that expand on the stories of the Old Testament. These stories come mainly from Jewish texts written between

250 B.C. and A.D. 125. The 39 books of the Old Testament (Hebrew Bible) did not comprise the sum total of Jewish literature. The Catholic and Orthodox churches, for example, preserve in their Bibles fourteen additional religious documents that were produced by Jewish authors (what Protestant Christians call the "Apocrypha" and Catholics refer to as the "Deuterocanonical" books). Beyond this collection, there are scores of texts that have also been handed down through the centuries—apocalypses, wisdom writings, poetry, retellings of portions of the Scriptures, as well as romances and histories. Some of these writings circulated widely among Jews around the turn of the era, and others were of interest only to a select few. We also have the works of two particularly prolific writers from the first century A.D., namely Josephus and Philo. Josephus wrote histories of the Jewish people from Creation through the Fall of Jerusalem in A.D. 70. Philo wrote lengthy interpretations of the "Five Books of Moses," the Torah. In what has been described as the most profound archaeological discovery of this century, a whole library of Jewish texts has come to light. The Dead Sea Scrolls contain many books that were previously available from other sources, including copies of the books of the Old Testament, a number of books from the Apocrypha (like Tobit and Ben Sira), *1 Enoch*, and *Jubilees*. The collection also contains many writings, however, that had not been seen by human eyes since the library was hidden away in the caves beside the Dead Sea in the first century A.D.

Within this wide array of early Jewish literature are many expansions and even revisions of familiar stories from the Bible. Many of these stories emerged as attempts to fill in the gaps of the biblical narrative, such as the life of Enoch, of whom the Bible says nothing except that he "walked with God" rather than dying a natural death. What a tantalizing invitation to speculate about the details of the kind of life that would lead to such a blessed end! Similarly, the Old Testament did not tell its readers all that they wanted to know about the life of Moses, or the lives of the prophets of Israel and Judah. Later traditions filled out Moses' story, telling of his upbringing in Pharaoh's house, his brilliant military career, and Pharaoh's envy and suspicion. The great prophets like Isaiah and Jeremiah fade from the biblical scene without any information about the "ending" to each of their stories. This, too, is provided by Jewish (and Christian) authors near the turn of the era.

Quite a number of stories appear to have emerged specifically as an attempt to deal with problems in the biblical story, or to answer questions about the biblical story. For example, without any explanation, God chooses Abraham to be the channel for blessing to all nations. What made Abraham so special as to receive this unique favor? Moses leaves Egypt as a fugitive from justice. Was the great lawgiver also a murderer? Joseph, a revered founder of two tribes in Israel, marries the daughter of an Egyptian pagan priest. How could Joseph have married an idol worshipper? Traditions emerged to provide answers to these questions and, in doing so, preserved the Jewish heroes from blame or explained what the Bible leaves unexplained.

A third motive behind these stories is the desire to answer basic questions about life in this world, or to promote certain ethical values, or support a particular way of keeping the Law of Moses that was so central to Jewish identity. Thus the question of how evil, violence, and oppression came to be so rampant in the world is explained by an expanded story about the giants, the offspring of angels and human females (see Genesis 6:1–4). The stories of the twelve sons of Jacob, among others, are expanded and retold as a vehicle for moral instruction, emphasizing the importance of harmony and solidarity among their descendants. In a period in which many Jews were attracted to the Greek

The angel Raphael instructs Tobias, the son of Tobit, about using fish for healing purposes.

way of life, questioning the validity of the Law of Moses, stories emerged that stressed the eternal force of that Law. It was not merely ethnic custom passed on since the time of Moses, but the permanent Law written in heaven and observed even by Noah, Abraham, Jacob, and Isaac—long before Moses.

Part II presents stories from the Apocrypha and related literature. For the Catholic or Eastern Orthodox reader, many of these will not really be "untold" stories of the Bible, for you will find Tobit, Judith, and the books of the Maccabees in your Old Testament. These stories will be unfamiliar to most

Protestant and Jewish readers, however. The books of Tobit and Judith were the "historical fiction" of the period, containing stories of piety, romance, and heroism. The First and Second Books of Maccabees provide a window into the tumultuous history of the second century B.C. The events recounted in these books made a deep impression on Jewish consciousness, and their impact can be seen in many of the stories told in Part I. Finally, we have included in this section Third Maccabees and the Letter of Aristeas. These two texts also belong to the family of "historical fiction," and tell stories that arose from the Jewish community in Alexandria, Egypt, the largest Jewish community outside of Palestine.

In Part III, we turn to stories about Jesus, his family, and his disciples. Early Christian writers from the second to fifth centuries A.D. filled in many gaps in the story of Jesus. These traditions focused particularly on his youth (the "lost years") and on the three days between his death and resurrection. A number of these works focus on the life of Mary or Joseph, showing the early church's interest in the lives of these specially favored parents and, in some cases, their relationship to their extraordinary son. Some of these writings became very popular, evidenced by the number of copies of ancient manuscripts that have survived. Many, however, served the needs and suited the sensibilities of only a small segment of the church.

Another group of writings, using the New Testament "Acts of the Apostles" as their model, fill out the details of the missionary activities and, in many cases, the martyrdoms of the apostles. Some of these, like the

Acts of Paul, the Acts of Andrew, the Acts of John, and the Acts of Peter, appear to have been available in written form as early as the third century A.D. While a number of them were rejected as heretical and unreliable by the main body of the church, a few were esteemed for a time as literature that could strengthen the faith and commitment of its readers.

Once again, these stories do not preserve what can be called reliable historical information, except perhaps in the barest sense (the fact that Paul and Peter were martyred in Rome, for example). The traditions tell us much more about what some early Christians thought about their founders, or wanted to believe about the lives and deaths of their apostles. Many stories had a moral lesson that would have been valued in the early centuries of the church, such as the defeat of magic before the true power of God seen in Simon the Sorcerer's fate. Tales of the martyrdoms of the apostles may have been circulated to encourage Christians facing fiery waves of persecution in the middle- to late-third century A.D. (though these traditions are also frequently regarded as preserving some reliable historical information).

This book, then, offers a collection of tradition and legend about figures known from the pages of the Bible. In the absence of reliable history, it is, ultimately, all we have. These traditions bear witness to the ongoing, vital interaction between believer (whether Jew or Christian) and sacred text—sometimes rewriting, sometimes expanding, but always returning to the stories and characters of the Bible for answers to life's questions, moral guidance, and encouragement to persevere in loyalty to God.

Adam and Eve

❖ ❖ ❖ ❖

BIBLICAL BACKGROUND

ONE OF THE BIBLE'S most-recounted stories, that of Adam and Eve, is found in Genesis 2–4. The way this infamous couple dealt with sin, shame, and personal relationships has been told by countless people for various reasons ever since Eve first bit into the apple. Whether as justification for the treatment of women, as a rationalization for thinking about nudity as shameful, or as a way to account for the origin of sin, this story has been used to serve a wide range of agendas.

The first couple was created by God, placed in the Garden of Eden, and instructed about what they could and could not eat. After enjoying some time in paradise, they were convinced by the serpent's arguments to defy God and eat from the tree of knowledge of good and evil. As a result, the couple became ashamed at their awareness of each other's sexuality and

Eve, tempted by a disguised Satan, reaches for the forbidden fruit.

were expelled from Eden. They were sentenced to labor for their food and suffer the pains of childbirth.

Their story concludes with the birth of Cain and Abel, the eventual murder of Abel by Cain, and the listing of the generations prior to the beginning of the flood. Numerous points in this narrative invite expansions and explanations. In particular, curiosity about what happened to Adam and Eve after they left Eden took over, and a host of stories were written.

Before looking at these extrabiblical tales, it should be noted that some cultural biases are at work in the text. Throughout the narrative, Eve continually repents the fact that she was responsible for their expulsion from Eden, and she is portrayed as gullible and weak. Such a portrait reenforces the view in the era between 200 B.C. and A.D. 200 that females were the source of all sin and a snare for males (see Sirach 9:3–8; 2 Corinthians 11:3; 1 Timothy 2:13–14). Adam, on the other hand, is presented as a pious man who takes his family responsibilities seriously, including the instruction of Eve on proper behavior.

THE FIRST LESSON: FOOD AND CLOTHING

This story begins after the expulsion from Eden. The book of *Jubilees* mentions the scattering of the animals, now deprived of the ability to speak, and the command that humans should "cover their shame" with clothing. Lacking any basic survival skills, Adam and Eve flounder about in search of the type of food they had enjoyed in Paradise.

Hunger, frustration over their plight, and the nagging of her own guilt drives Eve to suggest that Adam kill her in the hope that God would then return him to Paradise.

Such an unsatisfactory suggestion drives Adam to spend several weeks in fruitless foraging. Finally, he comes up with a plan. They must show God that they are truly sorry. Thus they will each spend 40 days (the usual number associated with penance or punishment) fasting. To draw God's attention to their repentant manner, they will remain silent, standing up to their necks in separate rivers: Eve in the Tigris River in Mesopotamia and Adam in the Jordan River.

It seemed that such an extreme measure would surely move God to be merciful. Even the fish are drawn to Adam to aid in his repentance. But all Eve attracts is another visit from Satan. After only 18 days, Satan disguises himself as an angel and entices Eve to leave the water to eat a feast prepared for her by God. She and Satan then go to Adam, who is absolutely astounded that she would fall for Satan's tricks again. Eve can only

THE FIRST FAMILY

Expansions of the Eden stories are most complete in the Latin text of The Life of Adam and Eve, (abbrev. *Vita*) dated to between 100 B.C. and A.D. 200, and the Greek version of the *Apocalypse of Moses,* (abbrev. ApMos) translated from an earlier Hebrew document no later than A.D. 400. The earliest existing manuscripts of these works date to the ninth century A.D. for the *Vita* and the eleventh century for the ApMos. A section in the second century B.C. book of *Jubilees* contains additional information about creation's "first family." There is also a gnostic *Apocalypse of Adam,* taken from the Nag Hammadi archives, that shows interest in these traditions within early Christian communities.

lament her failure and, in her self-misery, she asks Satan why he continues to plague them now that they have been expelled from Eden.

Satan's explanation is instructive: He is jealous of them. When God created Adam, the angel Michael instructed all the angels to worship Adam as the "image of God." Satan and many other angels were angered by this because they had been created before Adam. In their defiance, they challenged God's authority and threatened to set themselves up as lords of creation, "like the Most High." For this crime God cast them down upon the earth, where they determined to deprive humanity of all joy since they were denied the joy of God's presence.

THE SECOND LESSON: PAIN OF CHILDBIRTH AND CHILD REARING

Facing yet another failure, as well as the likelihood that Satan would be back to cause more trouble, Adam shows his determination to succeed. He resumes his forty days of penance while Eve separates herself from her more diligent husband. This separation is part of her "lying in" period prior to giving birth to their first child, Cain. Naturally, Eve is unprepared for the pain and cries out in her fear for Adam to help her. God does not respond to her plight until Adam prays for mercy. At that point Michael, 12 angels, and two "excellencies" gather around Eve and instruct her on giving birth.

Jubilees, a priestly document, makes more of this story from a legal standpoint than other, more narrative accounts. In this version, great emphasis is placed on the period of impurity brought on by Eve's pregnancy and childbirth. The blood associated with this event contaminates her and the child for up to 80 days, and she cannot touch anything that is holy during that time. Although she fails to complete her penance in the Tigris, the pains of childbirth, introduced at the time of their expulsion from Eden, create a specialized form of pain and penance for Eve and all future women.

THE FIRST MURDER

The only real addition to the story of Cain's murder of his brother Abel is found in a dream Eve has foretelling the event. She sees Cain swallowing all of Abel's blood, thus draining him of life. Alarmed, the parents

Cain murders his brother Abel in a rage of jealousy and anger.

try separating the sons, with Cain becoming a farmer and Abel becoming a shepherd. But this does not prevent the murder. A period of mourning follows the crime, but Adam's grief is lessened when he is told by Michael that they will be able to conceive more children.

Although cursed by God and forced to become a fugitive, Cain (according to *Jubilees*) marries his sister Awan and founds a city where he and his descendants can live.

THE THIRD LESSON: PAIN OF AGING AND DEATH

As Adam's days draw to a close, he takes his son Seth aside and tells him of his final meeting with God. While praying, Adam is whisked away in a chariot driven by the angel Michael and taken to an area of the "Third Heaven" known as the Paradise of righteousness. Here God, in the form of "unbearable flaming fire," sits amid his thousands of angels. Enthroned as judge, God pronounces sentence on Adam and all of humanity. Because Adam listened to Eve rather than to God, death will come to all humans. Adam accepts his fate by praising God, and then he is removed from God's presence. Michael aids his passage by causing the waters that surround Paradise to freeze long enough for Adam to cross over.

Having lived 930 years, Adam assembles all his sons at the "oratory"—the place where he made sacrifices to God. Later rabbinic sources tied the "oratory" to Mt. Moriah and the site of Solomon's temple in Jerusalem. As seen from the stories that follow, the "oratory" is also the place from which God took the clay to fashion Adam as well as the site of his eventual burial plot.

Adam's Version of the Fall

Lying on his deathbed, Adam tells his sons that he is in great pain. Never having seen anyone experience deathly pains before, the sons ask, "What is it, Father, to be sick with pains?" Adam is resigned to his own death, but he also realizes that he must pass on his life experience to his sons and answer their questions about the origin of pain and death. Thus he tells them his version of the Fall.

In this account, Adam describes how he was given charge of all the trees in the eastern and northern part of the Garden while Eve had responsibility for the western and southern portions. Two angels were set to guard them, but when they left their posts to worship God, the "adversary" took the opportunity to deceive Eve into eating the forbidden fruit. God's anger at this disobedience and Adam and Eve's attempt to hide lead him to inflict 70 plagues on humanity. Each plague attacks a separate portion of the body, racking it with pain and stealing its qualities.

Suddenly, Adam cries out in the midst of his suffering. Eve, unable to endure his affliction, prays to God to take Adam's pain and give it to her since she is the one who sinned. Receiving no response, Adam sends Eve and Seth to the gates of Paradise. There they are to act like mourners, prostrating themselves on the ground and putting dust in their hair. Adam hopes that God will have mercy on him, providing oil from the tree of life to ease his suffering.

The journey to Paradise is marked by a confrontation with a serpent that strikes out and wounds Seth. Eve scolds the beast for having the gall to attack "the image of God." Its response is to remind her that the enmity between Eve and himself, as well as her condition, are her own fault. Seth is angered by this insulting display of pride, and he commands the serpent to be silent until the Day of Judgment. The beast flees.

Once they reach the gates of Paradise, Eve and Seth perform their ritual of mourning for "many hours." The only response they receive is from Michael, who tells them that the oil of mercy will not be granted to any human until the time of Resurrection. They are instructed to return home where Adam will shortly die. To prepare his body for the grave, Eve and Seth gather nard, crocus, calamine, and cinnamon.

Eve's Version of the Fall

When Seth and Eve return, Adam is upset to hear that his son was attacked by the serpent. He again denounces Eve for bringing "transgression and sin in all our generations," and he charges her to tell their children the story of the Fall. This portion of the narrative follows the outline of Genesis 3, although there are a number of additions. Perhaps most important among them is the devil's use of the serpent. Genesis never explicitly mentions Satan, but the *Apocalypse of Moses* describes in detail how the devil first enticed the serpent to be his mouthpiece in deceiving Eve.

The serpent proves to be an able emissary. First he convinces Eve to discuss the forbidden tree in the midst of the Garden, raising her interest in it. Then, when she hesitates, the serpent offers to pluck it for her, so she opens the gate and lets evil enter the Garden. Finally, to insure that she will also entrap her husband, the serpent makes her swear an oath that she will give Adam a portion to eat as well.

Having eaten, Eve realizes her shame, fashions a skirt of fig leaves, and cries for Adam to join her. Like the snake, Eve now becomes the devil's mouthpiece, speaking his enticing words to Adam and causing him to eat. Almost immediately after Adam gives in, Michael's trumpet sounds, calling all the angels to witness God's judgment of Adam. The litany of charges and the terms of their life after Eden are much the same in this version as in Genesis. However, there are two attempts here by Adam to hold on to a portion of Paradise. First he pleads with the angels to intercede for him that he might eat from the Tree of Life. This request is rejected by God, although a promise is made that at the Resurrection Adam will have the opportunity to eat from this tree and live forever. Adam then asks for some of the fragrant herbs that grow in Eden so he may make sacrifices pleasing to God. This request is granted and thus crocus, nard, reed, cinnamon, and the seeds necessary for growing crops are transported to earth.

ADAM'S DEATH

At the point of death, Adam asks Eve to pray to God to receive "his own vessel" and to have mercy on him. She immediately begins a chanted recital of how

Naked and ashamed, Adam and Eve are forced out of Paradise.

she has brought sin upon all creation. Michael then appears, urging her to rise and see Adam's spirit brought to his maker. This is accomplished by the entrance of four radiant eagles drawing a dazzling bright chariot. They are accompanied by angels bearing censers that burn frankincense, and they call on God to forgive Adam, the one who "is your image."

Eve draws Seth up from his father's body to see the heavens open and the sun and moon darken, along with the angels praying for Adam's forgiveness. Once again a trumpet sounds, signaling God's willingness to grant Adam mercy. One of the seraphim carries Adam to the Lake of Acheron (known in Greek tradition as one of the waters of the underworld). Here he is cleansed before being transported by Michael, and accompanied by all the host of angels, to the Third Heaven where he will await the Resurrection.

God expresses sorrow over Adam's failure to obey his commandment not to eat from the tree of knowledge in the Garden of Eden. But he assures that all sadness will one day be turned to joy when the "seducer" is cast down and Adam is placed on his throne in glory.

Instructions are then given to Gabriel, Uriel, and Raphael to shroud Adam's body in three sheets of linen and silk. They are also ordered to take Abel's body from the place where Cain had hidden it and prepare it in a similar manner to Adam's. Both bodies are then interred "in the place from which God had found the dust" (traditionally the Temple Mount in Jerusalem). God calls once more to Adam and is answered by his spirit. Adam is told that although he is condemned to return to the dust, he will be raised in the Resurrection.

EVE'S DEATH

Eve must wait only six days before she too will die. Before giving up her spirit, Eve asks God to restore her to her husband since she had been formed from his body. Michael and three angels collect her body and bury it with Adam's and Abel's. This narrative provides the basis for a statute restricting mourning to six days and sets a model for the shrouding and burial of a body so that it will be prepared for the coming resurrection.

Following his mother's final instructions, Seth prepares stone and clay tablets that record the history of Adam and Eve's fall from Paradise. Since a warning had been made that humanity would be tested by God with water and fire, use of the two types of tablets insured that the story would survive either kind of catastrophe.

Enoch and the Giants

❖ ❖ ❖ ❖

Biblical Background

ONE OF THE MOST mysterious figures in the line of patriarchs who lived before the Flood is Enoch, the son of Jared. He was a seventh-generation descendant of Adam and Eve, through the line of Seth, and the father of Methuselah. The fact that he is said to have lived on the earth for only 365 years, a relatively short time considering the 969 years of his son, suggests something unusual. Enoch's life does not come to an end like other men. The text of Genesis 5:24 says that in his 365th year, Enoch "walked with God" and "he was no more, because God took him away." Only Elijah, the great ninth century B.C. Israelite prophet, shares this distinction of being taken up to the heavenly realm while still living (2 Kings 2:11–12).

Since so many aspects of his life, as well as his ascension to heaven, beg further explanation, it is not surprising to find extrabiblical descriptions of Enoch after God takes him away. Enoch was described as a righteous man to whom God revealed much about times to come and unknown places. In his post-translation "life," Enoch became both a source of information for his descendants and a shadowy figure lurking behind the scenes, recording the sins of humanity.

Who Was Enoch?

Enoch is described as the first man to acquire the skills of writing, mathematics, and astronomy. He is often referred to in *1 Enoch* as the "scribe of righteousness." He uses his skills to record the signs of the heavens, thus providing a calendar and establishing an orderly existence for human activity and for the worship of God, based on the agricultural year.

Like the prophet Daniel, Enoch receives visions and foresees coming events in the history of humanity up until the time of the Last Judgment. He then produces

Enoch did not die, but was translated into heaven after being on earth for 365 years.

a written testimony recording his visions. In this document, he also records the charges against the "Watchers," angels who sinned by impregnating human women (Genesis 6:1–4).

After accomplishing this task, Enoch is transported by the angels to the Garden of Eden. Here he continues the written record of humanity's evils that will form the basis of their eventual condemnation at the Last

Judgment. Because of his presence in Eden, this place alone is spared from the devastating waters of the Flood. And because of his continuous offering of incense on Mount Qater, one of the four sacred sites on earth (Eden, Qater or the Mountain of the East, Mt. Sinai, and Mt. Zion), the pollution of human sin will eventually be purged from the earth.

ENOCH AND THE GIANTS

One of the most bizarre stories found in the Bible is that of the marriage between the "sons of God" and the "daughters of men" (Genesis 6:1–4). This is generally taken as a brief explanation for God's anger with humanity and a reason for the Flood. However, the text provides so few details that its original meaning is unclear. Perhaps in response to this uncertainty, the writer

SOURCES ABOUT ENOCH

In addition to a brief mention in Genesis 5:18–24, traditions about Enoch are found in the extrabiblical books of *Jubilees* and *1 Enoch*. This latter work survives intact only in a few medieval Ethiopic manuscripts (the first was discovered in 1773), which had been translated in the fifth century A.D. from Greek editions. A section of a Greek edition, dating to the eighth century A.D., was discovered in a Christian grave in Egypt. Fragments of six copies of *1 Enoch*, written in Aramaic, have been recovered from Qumran, the site where the Dead Sea Scrolls were discovered in 1947. This suggests that its original form was either Aramaic, Hebrew, or a combination of these languages as in the book of Daniel. The book of *1 Enoch* was known to the New Testament writers, and it influenced Jewish and early Christian thought during the first two centuries of the Christian era (quoted directly in Jude 14–15).

of *1 Enoch* expands upon the Genesis account, attempting to explain how these "mixed" marriages and the birth of their giant offspring were committed as acts of rebellion against God.

In the first episode, a group of 200 angels, led by Semihazah and 19 other "chiefs of ten," makes a pact to seek out human females as their wives. They descend to earth at Mt. Hermon, north of the Sea of Galilee, to take an oath of solidarity. Each then proceeds to take a wife. This is considered rebellion against God's creation by the writer of *1 Enoch* in much the same way that Adam and Eve's rebellion is described in the *Vita*.

That evil is then compounded when each of the women gives birth. They do not bear normal children—instead they produce giants who eventually grow to heights of over 16 feet (300 cubits). These monsters consume all of the harvest, and then proceed to eat everything else they can get their hands on, including birds, reptiles, fish, animals—even humans. In their voracious feeding frenzies, they also consume blood, bringing down on them a great accusation and curse.

In the second portion of the narrative, evil enters the world through the spreading of "forbidden knowledge." Like Prometheus of Greek legend, the angels teach their wives skills and sacred information that had previously been reserved only for God and the heavenly court. For instance, the women were taught magic spells and the uses of medicinal roots and plants. *Jubilees* also mentions this instruction, but describes it as part of God's provision for humanity's survival.

The rebellious angels (this time led by Azaz'el) teach humans the skills associated with making weapons, jewelry, and cosmetics. This stirs up the humans' desire to engage in warfare and amorous pursuits, including adultery. The angels also teach various incantations, the secret knowledge of astrology, the interpretation of omens, and the means of manipulating people through knowledge of the movements of heavenly bodies. All this knowledge contributes to a desire for conquest and domination of others that will eventually promote universal warfare and violence.

The outcry caused by this turbulence, and the plea for justice from the earth, reaches the ears of God's angels Michael, Surafel, and Gabriel. They indict the "Watchers" for their acts of rebellion and call on God for instruction about how to deal with this situation.

God's answer includes warning Noah of the Flood (see the chapter on Noah, pages 30–33) and giving explicit instructions to Raphael to capture Azaz'el and imprison him within the earth where he will undergo severe torments until Judgment Day. The giants are set to fighting among themselves as a means of destroying them. Michael is then commanded to force Semihazah and the other angels to watch the destruction of their sons. Finally, they are to be bound up for 70 generations within the earth before being cast into the torments of fire at the Last Judgment. The elimination of these corrupting elements will usher in a period of perfection and peace for humanity. This most likely forms an apocalyptic vision of the end time rather than within the day of the writer.

After God judges the angels, the condemned rebels ask Enoch to intercede for them. Since they will not be able to raise their heads to heaven or speak prayers of repentance, they ask Enoch to write a prayer of supplication and present it to God on their behalf. God, however, will not relent since it was the angels' choice to leave heaven and defile themselves by fathering children. They had no need of wives in heaven, but their desire to create led them to be expelled forever, chained within the lowest reaches of the earth.

To further emphasize the fate of the angels to Enoch, he is taken on a guided tour of the earth and Sheol, the underworld. Here he witnesses the torment in which the angels are imprisoned and the sterility of an existence that is separate from God's glory. Like Dante's tour of Hell in the *Inferno*, Enoch asks questions of his angelic guide about each region he enters. And, again like Dante, he is eventually privileged to view portions of the heavenly domain, Jerusalem, and the Garden of Eden. All of this is recorded by the "scribe of righteousness" as a testament of God's power.

Noah and the Flood

❖ ❖ ❖ ❖

BIBLICAL BACKGROUND

THE ACCOUNT in Genesis 6–9 is a combination of at least two traditions, and it provides a fairly detailed narrative of the Flood. God became so angry with the violence that had overtaken his creation, he determined to destroy it all. However, because he is a righteous God, he warned the only righteous man of that generation, Noah, so that he could build an ark to preserve his life, his family, and a sample of all animal life. Yahweh (the Lord) is portrayed as a transcendent power, completely in control of the elements of nature.

ADDITIONS TO THE NOAH STORY

In the extrabiblical materials dealing with Noah and the Flood, the various writers do not seem overly concerned with the story line. They use the familiar episodes to reinforce the just nature of God's decision to destroy the earth and the evil that had engulfed it. The ark becomes a haven against the uncontrolled passions of the rest of the world, and the deluge is seen as the solution to the unbridled apostasy (backsliding from religious faith) that had afflicted humanity.

An interesting concern is expressed about young Noah in the fragment found in the *Genesis Apocryphon*. It is unclear whether Lamech's wife Bitenosh has given birth to her husband's child or has been impregnated by one of the rebellious "Watchers" (see the chapter on Enoch and the Giants, pages 24–29). This fear is based, as noted in *1 Enoch*, on the angelic appearance of this

Noah and his family, the only human survivors of the Flood, know the dove's return with an olive branch means the water is receding.

little boy: snow-white skin and hair, eyes that shine like the sun's rays, and a "glorious" face.

Naturally, any husband would be upset to think that his wife has not remained faithful to him. This particular situation is heightened further by the fact that so many women had fallen victim to the charms of the rebel angels. Bitenosh reminds Lamech of the pleasure they'd had together conceiving the child, recalling the "gasping of my breath in my breast." But neither this nor an oath to which she swears satisfies her husband's doubts. Lamech is so upset that he seeks out his father, Methuselah, and begs him to ask his father, Enoch, to confirm the truth. (Enoch is a man who has been translated to the heavenly realm and thus is privy to many secrets on earth.) Although the text of the Qumran fragment is broken, it seems clear that Enoch assures them the child will be a righteous man, not one of the ravening giants that were oppressing humanity. The narrative in *1 Enoch* confirms this, predicting the coming Flood and telling Lamech to name the child Noah. Lamech and his three sons are destined to survive because of Noah's righteousness.

The "Dream Visions" of Enoch include another premonition of the Flood. He tells his grandfather Mahalalel all that he has seen in his dream and is instructed to record these events and pray to God that not all flesh will be destroyed. Enoch then writes down all the prayers of that generation and calls on God to "sustain the flesh of righteousness" upon the earth. This matches up well with the decision God makes in the biblical account to warn Noah.

Thus when God determines to destroy creation with a deluge, the book of *1 Enoch* provides several descriptions of God's concern for the son of Lamech. In one instance, Noah cries out to the Lord that the earth "had

SOURCES ABOUT NOAH

The sources for additional information on Noah and the Flood include a first century B.C. text from Qumran, the *Genesis Apocryphon* (found in Cave 1 among the first of the Dead Sea Scrolls recovered), the book of *1 Enoch*, and the book of *Jubilees*. The differences between these texts and the Bible center on the repeated concern over the sin of the "Watchers" (described in the chapter on Enoch and the Giants) and the necessity to rid the earth of them. There are also fewer specific details of the Flood in these extrabiblical documents than in the biblical texts.

become deformed" with the violence and sin of all humanity. His ancestor Enoch then tells him that an order has been issued for the earth's destruction because of the spread of forbidden knowledge and the evil deeds of the "Satans" and other "occult powers." In the face of this impending doom, dramatized by a vision of the "angels of punishment" who were in charge of releasing the flood waters, Enoch assures Noah that he has been marked by God as one to be preserved.

Two other passages also mention God's warning to Noah. In the first one, God sends Uriel to caution Noah to "Hide yourself!" because of the coming disaster. Noah is then instructed on how to survive. In a later passage, Noah is told by God that his blameless life has entitled him to protection. Angels are said to be hard at work constructing an ark to preserve him and "the seed of life" from which will come a "substitute generation" after the Flood has cleansed the earth of the rebellious angels and their human counterparts.

The narrative in the book of *Jubilees* follows the biblical account fairly closely, though it always adds chronological detail. Thus the ark is constructed in "the 22nd jubilee of years in the 5th week in the 5th year." *Jubilees* adds Mt. Lubar, in the mountains of Ararat, as the site where the ark came to rest, but no mention is made of the use of birds as in Genesis 8:6–12. After making a sacrifice, there is a long expansion on rules against consuming blood along with the flesh of animals (compare Genesis 9:4–5). In later rabbinic tradition, the Noachide laws, as these came to be known, become the path to be followed by "righteous Gentiles" so that they too could enter heaven.

Abraham, Founder of the Jewish People

❖ ❖ ❖ ❖

BIBLICAL BACKGROUND

IN GENESIS 12:1–3, God calls out to Abraham, instructing him to leave his homeland and his kin. God promised to make of Abraham a great nation and a source of blessing to every nation. The Scriptures do not explain, however, what caused God's favor to rest upon Abraham in such a special way. Why did God choose Abraham for such an exalted destiny? Numerous explanations have emerged in Jewish tradition, all of which look in some way to Abraham's rejection of the evils of his peers and dedication to the God he did not yet know face-to-face.

ABRAHAM AND THE TOWER OF BABEL

An unknown author from the first century B.C. or early first century A.D. produced a sort of paraphrase of Genesis through 2 Samuel, interweaving narratives known from the Scriptures with other legendary stories about the biblical characters. This author, known as Pseudo-Philo since his work was attributed (wrongly) to the known author, Philo, links God's election of Abraham with Abraham's protest against the building of the Tower of Babel.

In this story, Abraham is one of twelve men (the list includes his brother, Nahor, and nephew, Lot) who refuse to assist in building the Tower of Babel. These men are thrown into prison and given a week to repent

Genesis 11:1–9 tells how the residents of Babylon decided to build a self-glorifying temple-tower that would reach into the skies.

or they will be burned alive in the furnace where bricks for the tower are being made. Joktan, the captain of the guard, knows that the God whom Abraham serves is powerful, so he seeks to free the men and preserve their lives. He sends fifty of his soldiers to prepare a hiding place in the desert and keeps another fifty standing by to escort the twelve out by cover of night.

When presented with Joktan's plan, eleven of the men are glad to go and seek safety, but Abraham decides to remain and entrust his fate entirely to God. When the citizens of Babel come to the prison at the end of the week, demanding the death of the traitors, they find only Abraham in the prison. Joktan says that the others broke out during the night, and he has sent 100 of his soldiers out to look for them. Abraham is brought to the furnace, but God destroys the brickworks along with 85,000 people. Abraham and the other eleven dissenters remain in Babylon and are not bothered again.

When God decides to bring his judgment upon the builders of the Tower of Babel, he also decides to lead his "servant, Abraham," out of Babylon to the land of Israel. This was the only land spared by the waters of the great Flood—a symbol of God's special protection of Israel, and also, perhaps, of the safety of Jews from the final judgment.

ABRAHAM'S REJECTION OF IDOLS AND SEARCH FOR THE ONE GOD

Many Jewish writers from the turn of the era speak of Abraham's rejection of pagan religion. Philo (in his book *On Abraham*) says that Abraham studied astrology while living among the Chaldeans, but that he rejected it, having received a perception of the One God. The first-century historian Josephus writes in *Jewish Antiquities* that Abraham left his native land

---

THE BOOK OF *JUBILEES*

Jubilees is an expansive retelling of Genesis 1 through Exodus 16, written in the form of a "revelation" to Moses on Mt. Sinai about "what was in the beginning and what will occur" in the future. It was probably written in Palestine between 161 and 140 B.C. The book has long been known from several Ethiopic manuscripts, a Latin text, and fragments in Syriac and Greek. The most important Ethiopic document can now be found at the British Museum in London. Numerous fragments of *Jubilees* have been discovered in the caves near Qumran, written in Hebrew, which was the original language of the work.

not only because of God's call, but mainly out of prudence, since hostility was mounting against Abraham on account of his preachings about the One God.

Two texts provide rather detailed stories about Abraham's search for true religion in his youth. The first is found in the book of *Jubilees*. The text seems to refer to the mass defection from observance of the Law of Moses (Torah) and the assimilation to a Greek way of life by Jewish aristocrats in the first third of the second century B.C. (see the Maccabean Revolt, pages 142–152). *Jubilees* responds to this trend by exalting Torah to the status of an eternal law, written in heaven, that was observed and taught in all its particulars even by the patriarchs Abraham, Isaac, and Jacob 400 years before it was written down by Moses. For example, Abraham observes the festivals of Succoth (the "Feast of Booths") and Pentecost (the "Feast of Firstfruits"), and he teaches Isaac about the proper way to conduct sacrifices and prepare sacrificial animals, projecting the laws of Leviticus back into Abraham's lifetime.

Even before adolescence, Abraham rejects idolatry, praying to God to keep him safe from the error of his family and neighbors. The boy shows great promise when, at the age of 14, he thwarts one of the demon Mastema's plans for making humankind miserable. Whenever people would sow seeds in their fields, Mastema would send crows to devour them before the farmers could plow the seeds under. So Abraham develops a tool that drops the seed on the ground at the same time it plows it under, and he teaches his neighbors to farm this way as well. Stories like this one bolstered the Jews' ethnic pride as contributors to civilization.

Abraham speaks with his father, Terah, about the emptiness of idol worship and urges him to worship the God who created heaven and earth. Terah admits to Abraham that he knows the truth, but he continues to worship idols out of fear of his neighbors, who regard the idols as true gods. When Abraham becomes an adult, he burns the shrine in which the idols are kept. His brother Haran, father of Lot, perishes while trying to save the idols from the fire.

Another example of Abraham's faith is displayed after Terah, Abraham, and their families leave Ur for the land of Lebanon. Abraham was watching the movements of the stars in an attempt to find out what sort of year it would be for rain and crops. During this vigil, "a word came into his heart" saying that the stars, sun, and moon were all in God's hand, and that rain would come according to God's desire. Abraham then speaks a prayer dedicating himself to God and choosing God and his kingdom over the error of the world. This conversion is the point where the biblical material can be introduced: Abraham, having professed his loyalty to God, is ready to be chosen by God, separated from his kin, and led to the land of promise. At this encounter, God also miraculously teaches Abraham Hebrew, the language that was spoken in Eden but had been lost since the Fall.

Another version of Abraham's rejection of idolatry and conversion to the worship of the One God is given in the *Apocalypse of Abraham*. Once again, the scene is set before Abraham's fourteenth birthday. Abraham goes to tend the gods of his father, Terah, and discovers that one, Marmuth by name, has fallen down. He gets his father, and the two of them lift it back into place.

WHAT IS AN APOCALYPSE?

The *Apocalypse of Abraham* was probably written in Hebrew or Aramaic near the end of the first century A.D. It has come down to us, however, only in an Old Slavonic translation and several Russian editions. These manuscripts are now housed in museums in Moscow and Leningrad.

There were many apocalypses written between 250 B.C. and A.D. 200. As a whole, apocalypses are revelations given to a human recipient through some supernatural figure (usually an angel) about the invisible world of God, angels, demons, the places for eternal reward and punishment, events of the distant past, and predictions concerning the final days.

It was common for the actual writer of an apocalypse to attribute the revelations to a distinguished figure from Israel's history or, later, to an apostle of the church. In situations where people might consider relaxing their commitment to the synagogue or church, these visions aimed to keep them loyal to their distinctive Jewish or Christian way of life. The visions frequently reveal that the angelic hosts share the values of the synagogue or the church (thus setting an example) and that God stands ready to execute judgment upon those who have not joined God's chosen people. Turning away from God or being morally weak would, therefore, ultimately prove destructive, so people were encouraged to remain committed to their religion. Apocalypses as a group tended to set everyday life within the broader context of the invisible world and God's future judgment, so that the readers would make choices for their everyday lives in light of that bigger picture.

But as they are moving the statue, the head falls off. Terah thinks nothing of it and makes another head for the statue. And since he already has his tools out, Terah makes five other gods and sends Abraham to sell them on the town road.

Abraham puts the gods in a saddlebag on a donkey and sets off. On the way, he encounters some Syrian merchants riding camels and begins to talk with them as they ride. One of the camels screams, causing the donkey to startle and throw off the bag, smashing three of the five statues. The Syrians purchase the remaining two on the spot, and Abraham throws the three broken ones into the river, watching them sink. Abraham begins to think that these are not gods at all, for they could not help themselves in the slightest way—his father was more of a god to them than they to him, for he made them.

A third episode clinches it for Abraham. His father had made a statue of the god Barisat out of wood. He tells his son to start a fire with the chips and cook dinner, so Abraham gets the fire going, warns Barisat not to let it go out, and goes in to get the food for the fire. When he returns, Abraham sees that Barisat has fallen over, the statue's feet already burning in the flame. Abraham laughs and proceeds to make his father's dinner. When Terah gave thanks to Marmuth for the meal, Abraham jokingly tells him he should thank Barisat for his meal, since he willingly gave himself up to cook it. Terah, however, takes this as a genuine sign and resolves to worship Barisat even more fervently.

Abraham finally confronts his father, saying that his gods are of less value than fire, which burns them up, or water, which covers them and extinguishes fire, which is itself of less value than the earth and sun, which dry up water! Abraham determines not to call any of these

At God's instruction, Abraham takes his wife, Sarah, and the rest of his family and wealth, and travels to the land of Canaan.

things "gods," but instead cries out wishing that the true God would reveal himself to them.

This sets the stage for God's calling out to Abraham, found in Genesis 12:1–3. In the *Apocalypse of Abraham*, however, God tells Abraham to flee from his father's house because God's wrath is about to consume it for the idolatry practiced there. Just as Abraham sets out, the house and everyone in it are destroyed by lightning. In both the *Apocalypse of Abraham* and *Jubilees*, Abraham's rejection of idolatry and exclusive dedication to the One God becomes an example for Jewish readers. These texts encourage Jews that, as they keep themselves free from Gentile error, they remain God's chosen people.

The *Apocalypse of Abraham* moves directly to the next encounter between God and Abraham. Genesis 15 tells of Abraham's sacrifice of a heifer, goat, ram, turtle dove, and pigeon. Abraham cuts the larger animals in halves and lays them out on the ground, chasing away the vultures. After nightfall, God appears to Abraham as a torch passing between the pieces, revealing to Abraham what his descendants will suffer in Egypt, and their eventual possession of the land of Canaan.

This episode could be easily expanded into a much more detailed revelation. In the *Apocalypse of Abraham*, an angel (described in terms of precious stones—something also encountered in the canonical Apocalypse of John) leads Abraham to the place for sacrifice. After Abraham prepares the animals, the demon Azazel flies down as a crow and tries to frighten Abraham, threatening that he will die if he remains on God's holy mountain. The angel rebukes Azazel and drives him off. Abraham chants a long invocation to God, who then appears in much the same way as Ezekiel 1 describes God's appearance (a fiery figure upon a chariot with fiery wheels, surrounded by strange, winged, multi-headed angelic beings).

God takes Abraham on a tour through the layers of the heavens to show him that there is no god in heaven besides the One God. God also shows Abraham the earth and its inhabitants, the places made ready for eternal punishment, and the Garden of Eden, which is reserved for the righteous. God goes on to show the destruction of the Temple in Jerusalem and, in what is

The Genesis Apocryphon

The discovery of the Dead Sea Scrolls in 1947 rocked the academic world. The *Genesis Apocryphon* was one of the first seven scrolls discovered in the caves near the abandoned settlement at Qumran. It was written in Aramaic sometime around the turn of the era. The document survives only in a fragmentary form, and most of its contents have been lost through the ravages of time on the parchment. The legible parts contain stories about the birth of Noah, the journey of Abraham and Sarah to Egypt, Lot's move to Sodom, an encounter between God and Abraham in which God repeats his promises, and the battle of the kings in which Abraham frees Lot and defends the kings of Sodom. The scroll is on display at the Shrine of the Book, part of the Israel Museum in Jerusalem.

no doubt a later Christian addition, the Messiah's rejection by some and the worship offered him by others. The vision foretells ten final plagues that God will bring upon people for their wickedness, as well as the deliverance of God's holy people and the punishment of their oppressors. This is part of a common trend in Jewish apocalypses and early Christian literature to see God's action in the "last days" as a grander version of the Exodus story.

Abraham and Sarah in Egypt

Soon after God first calls Abraham and he arrives in Canaan, a famine settles on the land, so Abraham takes Sarah, his wife, and all their people to Egypt until the famine is over. In the biblical story (Genesis 12:10–20), Abraham is seen in a less-than-flattering light. Abraham fears that Sarah's beauty might lead an Egyptian to kill Abraham so as to take Sarah for himself. He therefore instructs Sarah to tell people that she is his sister rather than his wife. Sarah's beauty does indeed catch the eyes of highborn Egyptians: Pharaoh himself takes her into his palace and treats Abraham very well on her account. God strikes Pharaoh and his household with disease, however, and Pharaoh learns (we are not told how) that Sarah is the reason. He therefore sends her back to Abraham and expels their tribe from his land.

This story leaves Abraham, the founder of the Jewish people, open to some serious accusations. Was he showing a paranoid distrust of the Egyptians, thinking of them as vicious and base? Wasn't it cowardly to expose Sarah to Pharaoh's bed just to keep himself free from the threat of danger? Finally, God had committed himself to Abraham, promising to make of him a great nation, blessing those who blessed him and cursing those who cursed him—so where was Abraham's trust in God?

Jewish authors, when retelling the story, have attempted to prevent "misunderstanding" of Abraham's character or actions by focusing on other elements of the story. Philo, for example, says nothing of Abraham's lie concerning his relationship with Sarah. Instead he discusses the lust of Pharaoh for Sarah, his use of a proposal of marriage as a mere disguise for lust, and the helplessness of Abraham to aid his wife, being a stranger in the land of a "lecherous and cruel tyrant." However, the author of the *Genesis Apocryphon* goes even further in defending Abraham.

On the night Abraham and Sarah enter the land of Egypt, Abraham has a dream about two trees—a cedar and a palm. Some men plan to chop down the cedar and leave the palm tree, but the palm tree cries out, "Do

not cut down the cedar, for we are of the same family."
The men then spare the cedar. Abraham takes this as a
warning of the danger Pharaoh will pose to his life on
account of his lust for Sarah. He therefore instructs
Sarah to tell people they are siblings, so his life will be
preserved. Abraham's fear and deception are thus the
result of a revelation that came to him in a dream, a
divine communication.

Three of Pharaoh's courtiers visit Abraham, and he
reads to them from the sacred books of Enoch. They
catch a glimpse of Sarah and return to Pharaoh singing
the praises of her beauty. Pharaoh's desire is kindled,
and he determines to possess her by violence. Pharaoh
comes for Sarah and is about to kill Abraham, when
Sarah cries out, "He is my brother." Abraham is therefore spared, but Sarah is taken away by force. Abraham
prays for God's intervention, so that Pharaoh's house
will know that God is Lord.

ABRAHAM'S *TESTAMENT*

The *Testament of Abraham* was written in Greek
sometime near the end of the first century A.D. It was
probably written by a Jew living in Egypt, since it shows
some relationship to other books (like 3 Maccabees)
known to come from Egyptian Jewish circles and because
the image of judging souls by weighing their deeds is a
peculiarly Egyptian idea. This text is noteworthy for its
emphasis on eternal judgment being carried out strictly by
weighing one's good and evil works—belonging to Israel
gives one no advantage over the Gentile at the final judgment. The major manuscripts are now kept in the Bib-
liotécque Nationale in Paris.

For two years, Pharaoh and his whole household are afflicted with disease. As a result, Pharaoh cannot fulfill his desire for Sarah. Harkenos, a courtier of Pharaoh, sends for Abraham so that he can pray for Pharaoh, but Lot replies that Abraham cannot intercede as long as Pharaoh keeps Abraham's wife in the palace. Pharaoh immediately sends Sarah back to her husband, and is healed by God at Abraham's request. The portrayal of the Gentile Pharaoh as a violent man, and the justification of Abraham's distrust of foreigners, reflects and reinforces the distrust of devout Jews toward the more powerful and threatening Greek world in the last three centuries B.C.

THE DEATH OF ABRAHAM

Genesis 25:8 records simply that "Abraham breathed his last and died in a good old age, an old man and full of years." Expansions on the death of patriarchs became a common feature of Jewish writings, particularly in the genre of the "Testament," the patriarch's deathbed speech and final instructions to his children. The *Testament of Abraham* is not a testament in the proper sense (Abraham never makes his will or gives final instructions to his children). Instead, it deals with the events immediately preceding his death. Abraham is not presented as a man who faces death courageously and dispassionately; rather, the seriousness and pain of death are made more real by his attempts to prolong his stay on earth and delay death as long as possible.

The day arrives for Abraham to die. Remembering Abraham's generous hospitality (compare Hebrews 13:2), God wishes to make the journey easier for his friend. So he sends the radiant archangel Michael, rather than the grim shade of Death, to escort Abraham to his eternal home. Michael greets Abraham without revealing his identity, and the two of them walk back toward Abraham's tent. As they pass a cypress tree, Abraham hears a voice say, "Holy, holy, holy is the Lord God who is summoning him to those who love him."

After visiting with Abraham for a while and seeing his hospitality and piety, Michael tells God that he cannot bear to announce the death of so righteous a person. God therefore sends the message to Abraham's son, Isaac, through a dream, which Michael can interpret. As Michael begins to speak, Sarah recognizes him as one of the three angels who announced the conception of Isaac so many years before (see Genesis 18:1–15). Abraham announces that he will not follow Michael to the grave willingly, and so Michael returns to heaven to seek further instructions.

Michael returns, offering Abraham a chance to enjoy any gift from God that he desires before dying. Abraham asks that he might see the whole inhabited earth, after which he will go willingly. He is accordingly lifted up in a cherubic chariot and begins to see what all the inhabitants of the earth are doing that day. When he sees certain people plotting murder, others committing adultery, and still others breaking into houses and stealing, he calls down curses upon them, and they die at once. God calls the tour to an abrupt halt, for God desires to delay the punishment of sinners so as to give them time to repent. He orders Michael to show Abraham the scenes of judgment and punishment so that he will repent for his lack of patience. The sight of the severe consequences of sin teaches Abraham mercy, and he pleads for the lives of those killed as a result of his curse. He also pleads for the souls whose destiny hangs in the balance because their evil deeds and good deeds are so evenly matched.

Returning from their tour, Michael again tells Abraham to prepare for his death by setting his house in order, but Abraham still clings to life and refuses to follow Michael. God therefore summons Death, who comes cringing into God's presence. At God's command, Death hides his face of decay and despair and puts on the appearance of a radiant angel. He is told to deal gently with Abraham, since Abraham is God's "true friend."

Even at the arrival of Death, however, Abraham refuses to follow. Instead, ever curious, he asks Death to reveal to him his true form. At the hideousness of the sight, most of Abraham's household servants drop dead (but are revived by Abraham's prayer). Abraham moves from room to room in his tents in order to get away from Death's presence, which has caused despair and heaviness to settle upon Abraham's heart, but Death refuses to leave him until he takes Abraham's soul. Finally, Death invites Abraham to kiss his right hand, and so receive supernatural strength. Abraham falls for this ruse; his soul cleaves to Death's right hand, and he is escorted by angels into the tents of the righteous in Paradise.

Later Christian traditions relate that the archangel Michael also visited Isaac and Jacob to prepare them in turn for their impending deaths. They respond more willingly than Abraham after taking their own tours of earth, heaven, and hell.

Jacob, Father of the Twelve Tribes of Israel

❖ ❖ ❖ ❖

BIBLICAL BACKGROUND

JACOB AND ESAU were rivals from the moment of their birth: Jacob clutched at Esau's heel in a struggle to be the first one born. Their lasting rivalry was fostered by their parents' favoritism, Rebecca preferring Jacob and Isaac indulging Esau. Throughout Genesis 25 and 27 Jacob jockeyed for first place above his slightly older twin, taking advantage of a famished Esau to gain his birthright of the firstborn. But that was not enough for Jacob, who later tricked his blind father into giving him also the blessing due the firstborn. It should surprise no one, then, that Esau wanted to kill Jacob, but it should surprise everyone that Esau, many years later, welcomed Jacob back with open arms. After all this, Esau really appears to be the more generous spirit, and a reader might be tempted to ask, "Why should Jacob be chosen by God, but Esau be rejected?"

JACOB AND ESAU

The book of *Jubilees* retells the story with additions aimed at answering this question, all of which present Esau in a bad light. Just as Jacob was the founder of the people of Israel, so Esau was seen as the father of the Edomites (later, Idumeans) who lived to the south of Judea. Relations between these groups were not always friendly, and the stories of Jacob and Esau reflect the later animosity between Israelites and Edomites.

Esau, exhausted from a day of hunting, agrees to give his birthright to Jacob in exchange for the stew his younger brother is cooking.

Just as Abraham's firstborn son, Ishmael, did not become the carrier of the promise—an honor that was given to Abraham's second son, Isaac—so Jacob supplants Esau in the line of promise. *Jubilees*, unlike Genesis, will not allow the reader to credit this merely to a mother's favoritism and scheming. Instead, it is the patriarch Abraham who selects his grandson Jacob to be the channel of the promises of God, blessing him twice before Abraham's own death. In fact, Abraham instructs Rebecca about Jacob's preferred status in God's plan and entrusts Jacob's care and promotion to her. In a particu-

The Importance of Endogamy

Endogamy is the practice of marrying within one's own clan, tribe, or race. It appears frequently both in Scripture and in these stories from the Intertestamental Period as a practice of central importance to many Jews. Marriage with non-Jews leads consistently to trouble for the Hebrews who enter the land of Canaan, usually because it opens the door to acceptance of idolatrous practices and worship of gods beside the God of Israel (as an accommodation to the non-Jewish partner). It even became the downfall of the great King Solomon, for his non-Jewish wives led him to all kinds of idolatrous practices. The result was the division of David's kingdom and, eventually, the complete loss of political independence.

When the Jews returned from exile in Babylon, part of Ezra's reform involved annulling all marriages between Jews and non-Jews, since these were forbidden by the Torah. In a "historical romance" found in the Apocrypha, Tobit goes through some considerable trouble to get his son Tobias to marry a person from his own clan (see pages 122–131). Endogamy became an important way in which the distinctiveness of the Jewish people could be maintained—if they were to resist becoming "like the Gentiles," this was a crucial line to draw.

larly moving scene, Jacob keeps Abraham company on his deathbed, lying on his chest as his grandfather passes away.

Jacob proves himself to be the more pious and devoted son in every way. Esau rejects his parents' preference that he marry a woman from among his own kin, and instead takes two wives from among the Canaanites. These foreign wives cause Rebecca nothing but grief with their idolatry and strange customs. Jacob, on the other hand, tells his mother how he has resisted Esau's constant urging to marry one of Esau's sisters-in-law, preferring to keep himself for the daughters of his uncle Laban. Moreover, when Esau moves away from home he takes most of his parents' flocks and goods with him, leaving his parents in need. Jacob, however, consistently sends supplies home to provide for his parents in their advancing years.

When Rebecca learns from a dream that the time of her death has come, she brings Jacob and Esau together to swear they will maintain peace between their families. Esau agrees to keep the peace with Jacob on account of their relationship by blood, but he asks Rebecca to make Jacob instruct his sons to be just and not overbearing toward Esau's children.

Later, the time for Isaac's death approaches. Isaac divides his property between his two sons, giving Jacob the larger portion, which would normally go to the firstborn. Esau agrees that this arrangement is fair, since he had sold his portion to Jacob many years before. When Esau returns to his own land, however, his children criticize him for yielding the larger share to Jacob. They determine to make war with Jacob and his sons, forcing Esau under threat of death to join with them. As the battle nears and his old injuries rekindle his hatred, Esau warms up to the idea. In the ensuing battle, however, Jacob kills his brother Esau with an arrow, and Jacob's sons force Esau's sons to surrender and pay tribute annually as a conquered nation. This grim ending to the story of Jacob and Esau is also told in the *Testament of Judah*, but is found nowhere in the canonical Scriptures.

Joseph, The Eleventh Son of Jacob, and His Brothers

❖ ❖ ❖ ❖

BIBLICAL BACKGROUND

GENESIS 37–50 TELLS the familiar story of Joseph, Jacob's favorite son. Because Joseph was spoiled by his father, his brothers became so envious of him that they sold him to a passing caravan of merchants and slave traders, reporting to their father that a wild beast had killed him. Joseph was taken to Egypt and sold to Potiphar, an officer of Pharaoh's army, who entrusted to Joseph the management of the household. Potiphar's wife sought to lure Joseph into her bed, but after being refused, she falsely accused Joseph of attempted rape and had him cast into prison. There his skill in interpreting dreams brought him to Pharaoh's court and eventually to the second most powerful position in the kingdom.

Joseph and his brothers became the patriarchs of the twelve tribes, and the rest of Israel's history is written with reference to these twelve patriarchs. Even Paul the Apostle identifies himself as belonging to the tribe of Benjamin (Philippians 3:5), and Jesus is spoken of as the "lion from the tribe of Judah" (Revelation 5:5). Of the personal lives of the eleven brothers of Joseph, however, not much is known. What extrabiblical traditions do exist can be found in the collection called the *Testaments of the Twelve Patriarchs,* the final words of each of the twelve sons of Jacob to their children.

POTIPHAR'S WIFE

Joseph came to be admired as a model of self-control, and later writers elaborated on the brief account in Genesis concerning Potiphar's wife's attempts to seduce him. A writing from the second century B.C. called the *Testament of Joseph* (one of the *Testaments of the Twelve Patriarchs*) claims to preserve the deathbed instructions of Joseph to his children. The document describes how Potiphar's wife repeatedly attempts to seduce Joseph over the course of seven years. At first, she acts toward Joseph as an affectionate mother, having no son of her own. But Joseph soon senses more than motherly affection in her touches. He admits on his deathbed how attracted he was to her, but says he nevertheless refused to betray Potiphar's trust.

Potiphar's wife visits Joseph often, pretending to desire to learn about his religion. Ultimately, however, she would only consent to put away her idols if Joseph gave in to her true desire. She plots to kill her own husband with poison so she will be free to marry Joseph, but Joseph foils her attempt. On another occasion, she tries to have her way with Joseph by sending him food that she has drugged. Joseph the dreamer, however, sees in a vision what Potiphar's wife is planning. He does not eat the food, but waits until she arrives later that night. She is surprised not to find him unconscious, and is ashamed by his knowledge of her plan. Then, in her presence, he eats the drugged food to demonstrate to her that no evil intention can overcome the self-control of the prayerful person. After some time, she assails him again, threatening to kill herself if he refuses her. Joseph calls her bluff, however, remind-

Potiphar's wife desperately clings to Joseph's garments. He is so eager to escape her advances that he leaves the clothing behind.

ing her that, if she did die, her husband's concubine would take her place and do away with her children.

Here the familiar story is told of how Joseph is so eager to escape temptation that he leaves behind his clothing in the clutches of the desperate woman. She then uses the garment as evidence against the young man and has him thrown into prison. In the *Testament*, her motive is purely anger at being spurned yet again. The historian Josephus, however, suggests in *Antiquities* that Potiphar's wife accuses Joseph out of fear that he will report her to Potiphar first. While Joseph is initially glad to be removed from temptation, the *Testament* tells us that even in prison Potiphar's wife pursues him, promising to have him released from his chains and torments if he will only yield to her.

These expansions on the temptation of Joseph are meant to heighten the reader's admiration for Joseph's ability to control his own desire. These stories also show that it is indeed possible to avoid adultery even in the face of relentless passion, "for these problems assail all humankind, whether in thought, word, or deed" (*Testament of Joseph* 10:4).

JOSEPH'S CONCERN FOR HIS BROTHERS' HONOR

In a second story, which goes back to the time before Joseph went to Potiphar's house, the *Testament of Joseph* shows how even the "silences" of Scripture were thought to be pregnant with meaning. When Joseph was sold into slavery by his brothers in Genesis, he does not say anything. Why did he not tell his buyers that he was the son of Jacob, the head of a large and powerful

Joseph was sold by his brothers to Egyptian traders, who in turn sold Joseph to Potiphar.

Bedouin tribe? At the very least, the Ishmaelite traders would have taken him back to his father out of hope for a reward, if not out of fear. As the storyteller who wrote the *Testament* reflected on this silence, he came to believe that Joseph kept silent about his parentage in order not to bring disgrace upon his brothers for selling him into slavery. In the *Testament*, the Ishmaelite traders ask Joseph about his origins after they purchase him and begin their journey to Egypt. Here he breaks his silence to say that he is in fact a slave, again so as not to bring shame on his brothers.

The Ishmaelites leave Joseph in the keeping of a merchant in Egypt, where Potiphar's wife first sees him. She reports to Potiphar a rumor that the young Hebrew was stolen from Canaan, and suggests that Potiphar punish the merchant and take the Hebrew boy into his house. Potiphar accuses the merchant of illegal activity and calls for evidence that the young man is indeed a slave by birth. At this point the Ishmaelite traders return to Egypt and find Joseph. They have learned that he is in fact Jacob's son and not a slave, and they tell Joseph of his father's grief. Though moved to tears to hear of his father, Joseph still claims to be a slave by birth in order not to confirm his brothers' disgrace. Philo also bears witness to this tradition in his *Life of Joseph*, adding that, during his whole captivity and even his tenure as administrator of the land of Egypt, Joseph never breathed a word about what his brothers had done to him. Instead, he always maintained that he was a slave from birth (this contradicts Genesis, for Joseph claims openly in 40:15 to be a victim of kidnapping, hence a freeborn person illegally subjected to slavery).

This episode, like the expanded story of Potiphar's wife, is also presented as a moral example. Joseph, in his *Testament*, says to his sons: "My children, look at what I endured in order to keep my brothers from shame. You, too, must love one another and patiently hide one another's faults." Joseph becomes a model to the Jews of the first century B.C. and beyond, not only because of his self-control, but also for his commitment to preserving the honor of fellow Israelites rather than avenging his personal grievances. The Joseph story as a whole serves as a constant reminder about the value of unity and harmony between Jews, an ongoing admonition to eliminate hatred and envy from among the descendants of Abraham. This solidarity is so important to the Jewish people that the book of *Jubilees* even suggests that Yom Kippur (the Day of Atonement, the most solemn and holy day of the Jewish liturgical year) was instituted as a day for Israel to mourn what Joseph suffered at the hands of his brothers, and to remember the importance of maintaining fraternal affection among Israelites. According to the author of *Jubilees*, violation of the bond of love and harmony among the "children of Abraham" was the chief sin that required repentance. Joseph's moral instruction in his *Testament* concludes with an instruction that resonates deeply with the teaching of Jesus: "If anyone wants to harm you, pray for him and do good for him, and the Lord will rescue you from every evil."

JOSEPH AND ASENETH

It was not just Joseph's resistance to the charms of the officer's wife that captured the imagination of ancient readers. They were intrigued not only by the woman Joseph rejected, but also by the woman he later married. Genesis 41 tells us that after Joseph's release from prison and rise to power in Pharaoh's court, Pharaoh arranged for Joseph to marry an Egyptian girl named Aseneth, the daughter of an Egyptian pagan priest. For later readers, the thought of one of the twelve patriarchs—one of the twelve founding fathers of the Jewish people—marrying an idolatrous Gentile woman was very troubling. This invited storytellers to create tales about the couple's courtship that, in part, filled in the gaps in the story and, even more importantly, explained how the mother of the tribe of Joseph was not, in fact, an outsider to God's covenant people. This story is told most fully in the romance *Joseph and Aseneth*, which was written in Greek in the province of Egypt sometime between 100 B.C. and A.D. 100.

Aseneth was the stunningly beautiful daughter of Pentephres, priest of Heliopolis. Many sons of noblemen, and even Pharaoh's own son, desired her as a wife, but she scorned every suitor. One day, while Joseph is on one of his routine trips through Egypt to collect grain during the seven years of abundance, he stops at the house of Pentephres to refresh himself. Pentephres is overjoyed that such a noble person would be his guest, and he seizes this opportunity to arrange a union between Joseph and Aseneth. When Pentephres presents this plan to Aseneth, praising Joseph's accomplishments, power, and chastity, Aseneth replies with her usual scorn. She refuses to be joined to a slave, a fugitive—one, moreover, who apparently tried to seduce his master's wife. When Joseph arrives and steps down from his chariot, however, Aseneth is at once cut to the heart with desire for him. She chides herself for her scornful words, and races downstairs to welcome Joseph. Pentephres invites Aseneth to greet Joseph with a kiss, but Joseph refuses to kiss the lips that have eaten food sacrificed to idols or blessed false gods. Aseneth is crushed, but Joseph, seeing her sorrow, prays that God will reveal himself to her.

Aseneth retires to her chambers, locks her doors, throws the idols of her gods out the window, and spends seven days repenting in tears and ashes. On the eighth day, Aseneth prays at length to the God of the Hebrews for forgiveness for her conceit and her idolatry. She asks for God's mercy and for the favor of being allowed to marry Joseph. After this, an angel appears to Aseneth, bidding her put off her clothes of mourning, dress herself in a new linen gown, and wash her face. He gives her the bread of life in the form of a honeycomb, which miraculously appears in her closet and restores itself after she breaks off a piece to eat. The angel declares Aseneth reborn and a refuge for those who will, like her, repent of idolatry, and then he leaves in a fiery chariot. Aseneth dresses in her bridal gown and greets Joseph, who arrives for his routine visit. After she declares her conversion, they kiss, announce their betrothal to Pentephres, and are married by Pharaoh himself.

As with all romances from this period, the couple does not yet live "happily ever after." Their love and joy, achieved with such difficulty, will be threatened once again. Joseph takes Aseneth to meet his father, Jacob, who now resides in Egypt with Joseph's brothers. As they return home, accompanied by Simeon and Levi (two of Joseph's brothers), Pharaoh's son catches sight of Aseneth, and his earlier passion for her is renewed. He summons Simeon and Levi, offering to make them rich and enviable in Egypt if they will help him win Aseneth. He bids them kill Joseph, while he himself will kill Pharaoh, his own father, who loves Joseph like a son. Simeon is enraged by this plot and wishes to strike down Pharaoh's son where he stands. Levi, being a priest and prophet, sees Simeon's thoughts and stamps on Simeon's foot so as to distract him while Levi announces their rejection of the plan in a more diplomatic way. Pharaoh's son then seeks the aid of Dan, Gad, Naphtali, and Asher, who were Jacob's sons by the servants of Leah and Rachel. He tells these four that he overheard Joseph planning to murder them after Jacob's death, since they were not his true brothers at all but only children of servant girls. This incenses Gad and Dan, who agree to ambush Aseneth and bring her to Pharaoh's son, and then kill Joseph while he is distracted by grief. Naphtali and Asher try to talk their brothers out of opposing Joseph once again, since God is obviously with him, but in the end they take their stand alongside Gad and Dan.

The plot is foiled by Benjamin who, riding with Aseneth, seriously wounds Pharaoh's son with a slingshot and drives off his supporters. Levi, always the seer, gains knowledge of the plot and rushes with Simeon and their forces to assist Aseneth. Gad and Dan pursue

Aseneth, at whose prayer their swords fall from their hands and disintegrate. The brothers, realizing that God fights for Aseneth as he did for Joseph, beg forgiveness from her as well as protection from Simeon and Levi. Aseneth calms Simeon's fury with a kiss, and Levi prevents Benjamin from dealing Pharaoh's son a final, mortal blow, since "it is not fitting for the worshiper of God to repay evil with evil" (*Joseph and Aseneth*). Instead, they bandage his wound and return him to Pharaoh who, learning of the plot and Levi's mercy, blesses Levi. But the wound eventually proves fatal, and Pharaoh himself dies mourning the loss of his son. Joseph reigns over Egypt as regent for 48 years, and then abdicates the throne to Pharaoh's youngest surviving son.

Joseph and Aseneth reinforces the importance for the Jews of marrying only those people who are committed to the One God. It also reassures the convert of God's special protection and highlights the value of not returning evil for evil as seen earlier in the *Testament of Joseph*.

REUBEN

The only story about Reuben found in Genesis that is not connected with Joseph's story is the brief statement in 35:22: "Reuben went and lay with Bilhah his father's concubine; and Israel [Jacob] heard of it." The *Testament of Reuben* merely adds a few details to the encounter. Bilhah gets drunk while Jacob is away visiting Isaac, his father, and she bathes naked where Reuben can catch sight of her. Reuben waits until Bilhah is asleep in her tent and, overcome by the sight of her unclothed body, lays with her. He relates, however, that he is punished by God with a painful ulcer in his loins for seven months after he has intercourse with his father's concubine. He goes to the brink of death, but is spared because of Jacob's prayers. Reuben's mistake serves as an exhortation to avoid sexual promiscuity. Waiting patiently and "wearying oneself in good deeds" until one meets the mate whom the Lord will choose is the lesson given to the reader here.

The book of *Jubilees* is also interested in this episode, particularly in the matter of Reuben's punishment. Why was Reuben not punished with death for violating the laws concerning incest? His survival is not to be used as an excuse for violating the law or supposing that punishment is inconsistently meted out, for the law of God had not yet been perfectly revealed at that point as it would be at Sinai through Moses.

JUDAH

In Genesis 48:22, Jacob tells Joseph that he will give him one portion more than his brothers of the land "that I took from the hand of the Amorite with my sword and my bow." Using this brief reference as a starting point, the *Testament of Judah* describes the military exploits of Judah and his brothers in battle after battle with the Canaanites. The *Testament*, however, is even more interested in the particularly troubled domestic life of this patriarch. Genesis 38 tells of his marriage to a Canaanite woman who bears him three sons. The first of his sons, Er, marries a woman named Tamar, but he dies without leaving an heir. Judah therefore sends his second son, Onan, to "stand in" for his dead brother and raise up offspring to his memory. Onan, however, knowing that the children would not be regarded as his own, begrudges Tamar his seed and dies under God's anger.

Judah is reluctant to give his last son to Tamar, saying that he, Shelah, is still too young.

After a number of years have passed, however, and Judah has still not provided a husband for Tamar, she devises a scheme by which to have children. When Judah goes to the city of Timnah to shear his sheep, he sees what he assumes to be a prostitute near a city on the road to Timnah. They agree on a young goat as a price, and Judah leaves his signet ring and staff as a pledge that he will send the goat later. Tamar conceives, and returns home. When Judah sends a servant with the goat, the prostitute is nowhere to be found, and the people of the city are not even aware of such a woman. When Tamar's pregnancy begins to show, she is accused of adultery and sentenced by Judah to be burned alive. But at this timely moment, Tamar produces Judah's ring and staff, and Judah realizes that he had intercourse with his own daughter-in-law.

The *Testament of Judah* lays the blame for this whole sordid affair on Judah's wife, the mother of the three brothers. Judah had met Bathshua, "the Canaanite woman," in the tent of Barsaba, her father, who was intent on joining his family to Judah's. Judah wanted to consult first with Jacob, his father, but Barsaba plied him with wine, showed him the size of the dowry, and finally brought out his daughter, who was enticingly arrayed in gold and pearls. Judah lay with her and took her as his wife.

Bathshua was distrustful of foreigners, and so had taken an instant dislike to Tamar, who, we are told in the *Testament*, came from Babylonia. It is because of Bathshua's conniving that Er refuses to lay with Tamar,

LESSONS FROM THE SONS OF JACOB

The *Testaments of the Twelve Patriarchs* contain reflections on events in the lives of each of the sons of Jacob, together with moral exhortations based on the pursuit of the virtues, or avoidance of the vices, displayed in the life of each patriarch. Many conclude with predictions of what will befall Israel in later centuries and also discuss God's final deliverance. These documents were written in Greek, probably within the Jewish communities of Syria (although Egypt is also suggested by some scholars). Since Syria is the last empire mentioned (the Seleucid dynasty, successors to Alexander the Great in Asia Minor and Syria), and since there is no clear reference to the Maccabean uprising of 166 B.C., it is likely that these texts were composed in the early part of the second century B.C. The combination of prophetic, priestly, and kingly roles in the *Testament of Levi* 18:2, however, has suggested to some scholars that the *Testaments* were written after 142 B.C., when Simon (a brother of Judas Maccabeus) held the kingship and high priesthood at the same time.

Joseph, now in a position of power, helps his 11 brothers.

and at his mother's command, Onan spills his seed on the ground rather than raise up children with Tamar. Finally, Bathshua finds a wife for Shelah while Judah is away, preventing Shelah from being given to Tamar. At this point, Judah calls down a curse on Bathshua, and she dies together with their last son. It is the Canaanite woman's plotting that leaves Tamar and Judah vulnerable for the union, which shames them both, and Judah bitterly repents of having "flouted God's command" by marrying a Canaanite in the first place. His story urges against the overuse of wine and the love of money, for it was these two things that inflamed his passion for a woman he ought never to have married (*Testament of Judah* 14–17).

LEVI

Levi is known in Genesis primarily for his leading role in taking vengeance on the people of Shechem following the rape of his sister, Dinah. Shechem, the prince of the city and son of Hamor, sees Dinah as she is exploring the area and takes her by force. He is so attracted to Dinah that he asks his father to arrange their marriage. Jacob and his sons agree to the union, provided that the Shechemites become circumcised like the children of Abraham. The Shechemites agree and their males are all circumcised on the same day. While they are recovering, however, Levi and Simeon dispatch all the males in the city and burn it to the ground. Jacob is enraged, believing that this incident will cause great trouble for him among the Canaanites, and he curses the anger of these two brothers on his deathbed. Indeed, Judah emerges as the leader of the twelve tribes because his older three brothers disqualify themselves in Jacob's eyes.

The book of *Jubilees*, however, sees the destruction of Shechem in a more positive light than Levi's own father does. Indeed, God's selection of Levi and his descendants for a perpetual priesthood is seen as a reward for Levi's zealous act for the honor of Israel. Levi and Judah together visit Isaac on his deathbed. Isaac blesses them, declaring that Levi shall serve in the sanctuary of God with the holy angels while Judah will be prince among the sons of Jacob, as it was written in the heavenly books. Levi is thus restored to a place of prominence alongside his younger brother. These two names become increasingly linked with Messianic hopes in early Judaism.

The *Testament of Levi* also relates this act of justice in a positive light. While tending the flocks of Jacob and lamenting the wickedness and deceit of humanity, Levi has a vision. In it, he passes through the layers of heaven, the lowermost of which contain the natural elements and angelic hosts that will be used in judgment. The uppermost layers contain the throne of God, who is surrounded by ever-worshiping angelic rulers and archangel priests who offer sacrifices on behalf of the righteous who have committed sins in ignorance. Here Levi receives his commission to be a priest to God, a commission that passes to his offspring until God himself comes to "dwell in the midst of Israel." At the conclusion of the vision, an angel commands Levi to exercise vengeance on the city of Shechem for the violation of Dinah's virginity. Although Jacob is grieved and angered by the slaughter, Levi knows that he has carried out God's just sentence.

Levi instructs his children to attend to God's Law wholeheartedly, and he predicts the disasters that will overtake Jerusalem because of the idolatry rooted in Israel. He predicts their return from exile, the restoration of the Temple, and their continued sinfulness until God finally brings judgment upon the priesthood itself. At that point God will raise up a new priest who will never have a successor, and who shall bring knowledge of God to the Gentile nations, remove the sword that blocked the way to Paradise, and allow the holy ones to eat from the tree of life. Later Christian scribes saw in this vision a prophecy of Jesus and included additional information to make the identification clearer for the readers.

SIMEON, ZEBULON, GAD, AND DAN

Very little is said about these four brothers apart from what is already found in Genesis. In his *Testament*, Zebulon presents himself as one who sympathized greatly with Joseph when his brothers acted against him, but failed to act or tell his father Jacob because he was afraid of his brothers. Together with Reuben, he begged them not to kill Joseph, and he stood guard by the pit to make sure Joseph was not harmed by Simeon and Gad, who bore him special malice. Dan confesses his envy toward Joseph, since Jacob loved Joseph best, as well as his joy at Joseph's demise. Gad explains his grudge against Joseph, relating how Joseph had informed Jacob that Gad was eating some of the choice lambs of Jacob's flock. Simeon confesses in his *Testament* to being furious with Judah for selling Joseph rather than allowing him to kill Joseph. God rebuked Simeon's fury by causing his right hand to wither for seven days. All four testaments exhort love and harmony among the descendants of Jacob, urging the readers to guard against the envy, jealousy, and hatred that dissipates the solidarity and strength of the Jewish people.

Moses, the Giver of the Law

◈ ◈ ◈

BIBLICAL BACKGROUND

PERHAPS NO FIGURE stands as highly revered in early Judaism as Moses. The *Testament of Moses* (early first century A.D.) concludes by calling him the "master of the word, faithful in all things, the divine prophet for the whole earth, the perfect teacher in the world." Given Moses' importance as the one through whom Israel's covenant with God was established, it is not surprising that his life would be the focus of many authors. Little is told in Exodus about Moses' upbringing in the palaces of Pharaoh, or of his activities before rejecting his adopted heritage in favor of his natural one. Later generations were happy to supply a wealth of suggestions for these "lost years" of Moses, as well as to enhance the stories about Moses' parents and infancy. These writers were also frequently concerned with downplaying those biblical stories that might be seen as blemishes on the character of Moses. For example, Exodus explains that Moses first left Egypt as a fugitive wanted for murder. Several extrabiblical writers present alternative explanations that put Moses in a more positive light.

THE FAITH OF AMRAM AND JOCHEBED, MOSES' PARENTS

Exodus 1–2 tells us that, sometime after Joseph's death, his benefits to the people of Egypt were forgotten.

In fact, the Egyptians began to look upon the greatly multiplying descendants of Jacob as a threat. As the population of Hebrews grew, the Egyptians reasoned, they might attempt to take over the land. Fearing their numbers, the reigning Pharaoh began to afflict the Hebrews with hard labor, setting brutal taskmasters over them, and gradually enslaving them. When this did not curb their growth, he enlisted the help of midwives who assisted in the births of Hebrews, ordering them to allow females to live but to kill the males. The midwives, themselves worshipers of the God of Israel, did not carry out Pharaoh's instructions, so Pharaoh made his private instructions to them a public law.

A Hebrew from the tribe of Levi took a wife from the same tribe. They conceived a son, whom they sheltered for three months. At the end of that time, the mother made a basket of reeds and set the baby adrift in the Nile, setting her daughter to watch it and see what became of the child. Pharaoh's daughter found the child when she came to bathe, and she took him into her own house, calling him "Moses" (which means "drawn out of the river").

Moses' parents, though left unnamed in the opening of Exodus, become heroes of faith in their own right (see Hebrews 11:23), and at least one author has left a fuller testimony to their courage. In his *Biblical Antiquities*, Pseudo-Philo reports that the plot of the Egyptians was even more devious than what is recorded in Exodus. They wish to kill the male children and raise up the females as wives for Egyptian slaves and breeders of more slaves. Far from being merciful, allowing the daughters to live reflects an intent just as evil as the

Pharaoh's daughter, with her maids, finds Moses. Although the crying infant is a Hebrew, Pharaoh's daughter decides to keep him.

slaughter of the sons. The Hebrew elders plan to meet this threat by avoiding all sexual intercourse with their wives, so as not to increase their sorrows. But Amram, a Levite, declares his trust in God's promises to protect and exalt the people of Abraham, and so he determines to do his part to perpetuate the race. Amram's faith pleases God, who determines to make of Amram's son a channel for God's wonders, deliverance, and law.

Amram marries Jochebed and they have a son, whom they name Aaron, and a daughter, whom they name Miriam. God announces to Miriam through a dream that her second brother, yet unborn, will lead the Hebrews to deliverance. The rest of the story in *Biblical Antiquities* continues much as it does in Exodus, except for the detail that Moses is born circumcised, showing that he has been marked by God for the covenant people even from his mother's womb.

In his *Antiquities*, Josephus adds an intriguing twist to Moses' story. He speaks of a prophecy among the priests of Egypt concerning the birth of a boy who would bring shame upon the rulers of Egypt and deliver the Hebrew slaves from bondage. In this version it is this prophecy, rather than the need for population control, that prompts Pharaoh to order the death of every newborn Hebrew male. Pharaoh hopes thus to cut off the Deliverer before he grows to become a threat. Amram, knowing that his wife is pregnant, prays to God for help. God reveals to him that his own child will be this savior and assures him that God will keep him safe. The child would be raised in a marvelous manner, deliver the Hebrews, and be remembered forever. The parallels between Josephus (writing in about A.D. 90) and Matthew's account of Jesus' birth (written sometime between A.D. 60 and 90) are striking indeed.

MOSES, PRINCE OF EGYPT

Nothing more is mentioned in Exodus about Moses' youth after he is adopted by Pharaoh's daughter as an infant. The next biblical episode shows Moses as a grown man, defending a Hebrew who was being beaten by an Egyptian taskmaster, and then fleeing the land as a murderer. What did Moses, whose adult years were full of miracle and drama, do in his youth?

According to Josephus, Pharaoh's daughter, Thermuthis, presents the three-year-old Moses to Pharaoh and tells her father the story of his being found by chance in the river. She suggests that Moses become the heir to the throne of Egypt, since there is as yet no other heir apparent. Pharaoh embraces Moses, signaling his acceptance of the boy as his own heir, and sets the crown of Egypt upon his head. Moses, however, throws the crown down to the floor and begins, playfully, to trample it underfoot. Pharaoh takes this as a bad omen, and the priest who had originally prophesied the coming of a child who would be a danger to Egypt identifies Moses as that child. Moses escapes being killed only because of Thermuthis's speed in hiding the child from Pharaoh, who was reluctant, anyway, to eliminate the only suitable heir to the throne.

Many years later, the Ethiopians ravage the southern provinces of Egypt. The Egyptian army tries to repel them, but are only pushed back to the north themselves. At this critical point, an oracle names Moses as Egypt's only hope. Pharaoh, his priests, and his courtiers approach Thermuthis concerning the whereabouts of her son. After she secures oaths from her father that he will not attempt any treachery, she gives Moses over to them to serve as general of the army. Moses devises a strategy for crossing a snake-infested desert path with his army to surprise the Ethiopians on their flank. Driving them out of Egypt, he besieges the Ethiopian forces and the crown princess, Tharbis, in one of their fortresses. During the siege that follows, Tharbis, observing Moses' courage and his intelligence in the art of war, falls in love with him. She negotiates a treaty with Moses, offering herself as his bride, so ending the enmity between their peoples.

When Moses returns after achieving such a stunning victory, Pharaoh is stricken with jealousy. Pharaoh's courtiers fan the embers of envy into a flame of fury, stirring up suspicions that Moses is plotting to overthrow him. Remembering the old prophecy, Pharaoh consents to have Moses killed. Word of this reaches Moses' ears, and he flees to Midian. Josephus omits all mention of Moses' murder of an Egyptian as the precipitating cause for his flight—he is no longer a criminal fleeing justice, but a courageous general and prince fleeing envy and treachery.

Artapanus, an Egyptian Jewish historian from the third or second century B.C., also seeks to defend Moses against the charge of murder. In his version, the

Pharaoh (named Chenephres), disappointed that Moses did not die in battle, sends out an assassin against him. Moses, learning of the plot, flees to Arabia. On the road, he meets the assassin and kills him innocently in self-defense.

Having received a commission from God, Moses determines to lead an army of Arabians against Egypt in order to free the Hebrews from slavery. He first consults his brother Aaron, who is living in Egypt with the Hebrews. When Pharaoh learns that Moses has returned and what Moses intends, he throws him into prison. That night, the prison doors fly open and the guards are struck down, some by death, some by deep sleep. Moses walks freely into Pharaoh's bedchamber. Pharaoh asks the name of this God who has freed Moses and sent him, and faints upon hearing it pronounced. The plagues and events known from Exodus follow in both Josephus' and Artapanus' accounts without significant additions.

Underscoring Moses' advancement in Egyptian government served to heighten the nobility of his choice to side with the Hebrews. He becomes the supreme example to Jews and Christians alike of choosing the advantages of solidarity with the people of God rather than enjoying the pleasures of wealth or power cut off from God (see Hebrews 10:24–26).

Ezekiel the Tragedian, a playwright from the second century B.C., retells the story of the Exodus as a drama. This play, which survives only in fragments, adds a scene after Moses' flight from Egypt that speaks of Moses' importance in the plan of God. Moses has a dream in which he sees the throne of God, and upon the throne a human figure with a scepter and crown. God vacates the throne and allows Moses to sit on it, giving him the scepter and crown. Moses then rules over the world as God's vizier. This tradition bears witness to the esteem in which Moses was held in the Intertestamental Period, and the conviction that God ruled and judged the world through Torah, the law that was given through Moses.

THE DEATH OF MOSES

Both Philo and Josephus, believing that Moses actually wrote the first five books of the Bible, claim that Moses prophesies about his own death (writing about it himself in Deuteronomy 34). Moses dies outside the land of Israel, only seeing the promised land but not setting foot upon it, as punishment for a single act of disobedience recorded in Numbers 20:4–13. After forty years of seeing God's provision for them, the Hebrews nevertheless complain yet again to Moses about needing water, accusing him of bringing them to the desert to die. God instructs Moses to stretch out his hand and speak to a rock, which will pour forth water. Moses, however, yells at the people, "Listen, you rebels! Shall we bring out water for you out of this rock?" (Numbers 20:10). Moses struck the rock twice, and water flowed out in abundance. God said to Moses, however, that because Moses did not trust God or treat God as holy in that incident, Moses would not lead the people into the promised land. God himself buries Moses, and his burial place remains unknown.

To think that Moses failed to enter the promised land because of his own sin was too much for some writers. One author (Pseudo-Philo) wrote that Moses is

Moses gazes at the promised land that he is not allowed to enter.

prevented by God from entering not because of an act of disobedience; rather, God wanted to spare Moses from seeing the idols in the land of Canaan that the Israelites would begin to worship and by which they would be led astray, thus bringing Moses' work to near ruin. When Moses dies on Mount Nebo, God sets Moses' staff in his own presence as a reminder to spare Israel and not destroy it utterly when it sins. The staff would remind God of Moses' constant mediation for the people—of the many times when God spared Israel from destruction for Moses' sake while he lived. So God would continue to show patience toward Israel now that Moses was dead.

The New Testament letter of Jude includes a brief reference to a dispute between the archangel Michael and the devil over Moses' body. Jude assumes that his readers will know this story, but the tradition has been lost to posterity, along with the *Assumption of Moses*, the text that is believed to contain the full narrative to which Jude refers. Their argument appears not to have involved the destiny of Moses' soul, but merely the disposal of the body, which the devil desired to use, in the ultimate act of irony, as an object of idolatrous worship to lead Israel astray from the worship of the One God.

ADDITIONAL STORIES ABOUT MOSES

Other traditions about Moses also exist. In his *Life of Moses*, Philo relates how Pharaoh's only daughter, being childless, intends to present Moses as her natural son. She pretends to be pregnant while Moses is being nursed by the Hebrew woman hired for the task (Moses' natural mother, as it happens). Moses thus becomes heir apparent to the throne of Egypt. He is educated in arithmetic, geometry, music, hieroglyphics, Aramaic, and astronomy. After learning the truth of his parentage, Moses is attracted to the culture and learning of his natural kin while remaining grateful to his adoptive family. Nevertheless, when Pharaoh implements his plan to enslave the Hebrews, Moses grows restless and impatient with the new policy. He frequently stands by the taskmasters, urging them to show mercy and not be so zealous to inflict pain. Once, when an Egyptian responds to his pleas by becoming even more fierce, Moses kills the man. Pharaoh is enraged at the murder, but more upset that his own daughter's son would not support his policy. Courtiers fuel Pharaoh's suspicion and fury with tales of conspiracy, and so Moses is forced to flee for his life.

Artapanus credits Moses with teaching the Egyptians the alphabet and the art of making boats, and also with inventing new construction equipment, weapons, and irrigation instruments. Eupolemus (a historian writing in 158/7 B.C.) also credits Moses with teaching the alphabet, but in this case it is to the Jews (and thence to the Phoenicians, from whom the Greeks learned letters) rather than from the Egyptians.

The Judges of Israel

❖ ❖ ❖ ❖

BIBLICAL BACKGROUND

THE BOOK OF JUDGES describes a world of chaos and anarchy. After settling in the land of Canaan, the Israelite tribes found themselves surrounded by enemies. These nations controlled most of the fertile lands, dominating the economy and forcing the struggling Israelite towns and villages to "pay tribute" by giving up a portion of their harvest. Attempts at military reprisal were stymied by Canaanite walled cities, armies led by chariot squadrons, and soldiers equipped with iron weapons. This period of oppression was a punishment placed on the Israelites by God, who was angered by their failure to obey the covenant. Only when they repented was he willing to raise up a Judge, who would temporarily free a portion of the land from their enemies. However, these Judges often had to deal with contentious fellow Israelites. Plus, once the Judge passed from the scene, the people returned to their sin and were again left to their oppressors by an angry God.

THE UNTOLD STORY OF KENAZ

Among the more shadowy figures in the Book of Judges is Kenaz, the father of Othniel (Judges 3:9–11). While his son is described in much the same way as other Judges, the only detailed information on Kenaz is found outside the Bible. In Pseudo-Philo's colorful narrative, Kenaz has life and death authority over all the tribes, and he functions as a super-human military leader, in much the same vein as Samson.

The story of Kenaz begins with the Israelites' concern that their community is harboring men who have committed heinous sins, violating the covenant with God. The Israelites know that God will not support them in his role as Divine Warrior if these men are allowed to live. However, rather than take the initiative themselves to find the culprits, they first cast lots to determine a successor to Joshua, who will take the responsibilities of leadership.

Kenaz, from the family of Caleb, is chosen, and he immediately makes a speech reaffirming the people's strict adherence to the law, much like that of Joshua (Joshua 24:2–15). Lots are then cast for each of the tribes, revealing the lawbreakers—a total of 6,110. When Kenaz demands that they confess and thus gain some hope of God's mercy at the resurrection, a spokesman from among them suggests that he ask each man in turn what his sin was.

The list of offenses is very grave indeed. It includes all sorts of idol worship, the consulting of demons, child sacrifice, profaning the Sabbath, and questioning the divine origin of the law. The lawbreakers also have in their possession seven jewel-encrusted sacred images and a set of books containing incantations for foreign gods. These had been taken from the Amorites, one of their enemy neighbors.

God commands that all these offenders be taken to the Valley of Kidron, near Jerusalem, and be burned along with all of their possessions (see the execution of Achan in Joshua 7:16–26). The jewels and sacred books are a problem that only God can deal with—their power has been used to invoke other gods and can only be neutralized through divine intervention. Kenaz proves this to himself by first casting the stones into a fire and seeing them extinguish the flames. He then attempts to smash them with an iron sword, but the blade melts when it comes in contact with the jewels.

Seeing the power of these possessions, Kenaz follows God's instruction to place them on top of a mountain (either at Shechem or Shiloh) and then perform a huge sacrifice and feast to celebrate the purification of the people. God provides a new set of powerful jewels, one for each tribe, and instructs Kenaz to place them in the ark of the covenant, along with the tablets containing the Ten Commandments. They are to remain there until Solomon builds the Jerusalem temple, at which time they will be displayed before the cherubim in the Holy of Holies. A prediction is then made that eventually God will have to retrieve the stones before a sinful Jerusalem falls to its enemies. However, they will eventually resurface to light the path of the righteous.

Having cleansed the Israelites of all corrupting elements, Kenaz leads them to war against the Amorites.

SOURCES ABOUT KENAZ AND DEBORAH

The principal source for the stories of Kenaz and Deborah discussed here is the work by Pseudo-Philo, titled in Latin *Liber Antiquitatum Biblicarum*. It was composed in Hebrew some time prior to the destruction of the Jerusalem temple in A.D. 70 and perhaps as early as 135 B.C. Subsequently, it was translated into Greek and then into Latin. Existing manuscripts all date to the medieval period (the oldest is from the 11th century). Additional material is also found in the first century A.D. Jewish historian Josephus' *Antiquities of the Jews.*

With an army that is vastly outnumbered, Kenaz wins two battles in which over a million enemy soldiers are killed. Despite these monumental victories, a group of 35 men begins spreading rumors that Kenaz is letting the common soldiers die in battle while he dallies with his wives and concubines. The men are immediately arrested for spreading dissent, and imprisoned while Kenaz performs a feat of military skill to quiet all his detractors.

Taking only 300 horsemen, Kenaz prepares to attack the Amorite camp. He leaves his men, proposing to scout the enemy emplacement. However, he prays to God to grant him an extraordinary victory. He will enter the enemy camp alone and he will leave it up to God to decide if he is worthy enough to become the incarnation of God's wrath. Kenaz asks that when he draws his sword it will shine so brightly that the Amorites will be thrown into confusion.

The Amorites recognize their enemy as he comes within sight, and they see this as their opportunity to

THE ANCIENT "COIN TOSS"

Casting lots or the use of the Urim and Thummim were common forms of divination in the ancient world. They were used like we use a coin toss to make decisions or determine someone's fate. The assumption was that God would answer questions or point out a direction depending on how the lot fell. Other forms of divination used in the ancient Near East included examining the flight of birds or cloud formations, noting the position of the stars and planets, and even the study of a freshly removed sheep's liver.

slay him and recapture their seven sacred images. However, Kenaz's sword shines "like a lightning bolt" and he is "clothed with the spirit of power" (compare Samson in Judges 15:14–16) and begins mowing down the Amorites. He is aided by two angels who give him super-human strength and bear up his arms when they tire (compare Moses in Exodus 17:8–13). All told, 45,000 Amorites are slain.

When his 300 men awake from their night's sleep and find a battlefield filled with bodies, they praise God for this sign of deliverance. This, of course, reenforces Kenaz's leadership position, and he immediately orders the execution of the men who had questioned his authority (compare Moses in Numbers 16:1–35).

Kenaz will rule the Israelites for 57 years. In his final days, the priest Phinehas reminds Kenaz and the elders that Israel will eventually turn away from God. Kenaz and the others lament, asking God to spare his flock. During this period of supplication, Kenaz is infused with the holy spirit, and he prophesies (compare Numbers 24:17). His prophetic vision describes a period of 7,000 years in which humanity will dwell upon the earth before they are at last transformed. His final words are similar to those of the prophet Balaam (Numbers 23:10), saying that all people should remain upright until death, and not be corrupted by the sins of the world. As with Moses, the people mourn Kenaz for thirty days (Deuteronomy 34:8).

THE STORY OF DEBORAH

Deborah is the only female Judge in the Bible (Judges 4–5). Her story, like that of most of the other judges, involves freeing people from the oppression of an enemy nation. Deborah predicts a victory over the Canaanite King Jabin and his general, Sisera, but the timidity of the Israelite general Barak leads her to also say that the victory will come at the hands of a woman. Ultimately, this prediction comes true when the Kenite woman Jael slays the Canaanite general Sisera.

Josephus and Pseudo-Philo provide some additional details to flesh out this story. However, Josephus gives Deborah's role little attention, preferring to highlight the actions of general Barak and of the Kenite woman Jael. Like Josephus, Pseudo-Philo portrays Deborah as a prophetic figure, but in addition she is allowed to serve as a moralist, calling the people back to the covenant and presenting herself as an authoritative spokesperson for God. In this account, her choice as Judge comes after a period of seven days of fasting when the people realize they must repent to gain God's favor. She recites many of the saving acts and miraculous events God had performed on their behalf, and she reminds them how they had forgotten all this and the direction of Moses, Joshua, and Kenaz as soon as these leaders had died.

In Pseudo-Philo's description of the battle against Sisera, there is no mention of Barak's reluctance to go without Deborah (found in Josephus and Judges 4:8). Nor is there any mention of the tribes who refused to join her campaign (Judges 4:8–10). Rather, the prediction here is that Sisera will fall at the hands of a woman because of his boast to divide up Israel like spoils. God uses the radiance of the stars to burn up Sisera's army, killing over 8 million of the enemy.

Pseudo-Philo's version depicts Jael as a seductress, enticing Sisera to her tent and casting rose petals on her

Jael, a Kenite woman, kills the Canaanite general Sisera by driving a stake into his head. This fulfills Deborah's prediction of victory.

bed as a suggestion of pleasure to come. She repeatedly asks God for a sign that he will aid her, acknowledging Yahweh as the true God. When she receives the sign, she gives Sisera a potion of milk and wine to make him sleep. Even when she pushes the sleeping general off the bed, he does not awake. Only when Jael drives a stake (an iron nail in Josephus' version) through his temple does Sisera speak in despair, saying that he is dying "like a woman." When Barak finds the body of his enemy, he blesses Jael, then cuts off Sisera's head and sends it to Sisera's mother, taunting her for the Canaanite's hope of despoiling Israel. Josephus, who treats Deborah as a secondary character, ends his account with Barak's capture of the city of Hazor.

In the biblical narrative as well as in Pseudo-Philo, however, Deborah continues to be a major figure. She responds to these events with a hymn of praise that again recites the epic history of the Israelites and their covenant with God. In particular, she notes the unique event of the stars unleashing their power, at God's direction, to vanquish an enemy.

After serving the Israelites for 40 years, Deborah gathers the people for her last words. She enjoins them to live their lives in obedience to the law since no repentance is possible after death. When they ask her spirit to remember them after she dies, Deborah tells them that after death no spirit has the power to pray for or in any way aid the living. This concept is a direct attack on the popular forms of ancestor worship that had existed in the area for thousands of years. Following her death, the people mourned Deborah for an unprecedented 70 days.

JEPHTHAH'S DAUGHTER

The very strange case of the unnamed daughter of Jephthah appears in Judges 11:29–40. The judge Jephthah makes a vow that if God will give him a victory over the Ammonites he will sacrifice whoever comes out of his door to greet him on his return. As fate would have it, Jephthah's only child, a daughter, comes to welcome her victorious father. He is reluctant to fulfill his vow, but she convinces him it is necessary. She only asks for two months delay to wander the mountains and "bewail" her virginity. She then returns, and her father "did with her according to the vow he had made."

The lack of details about the sacrifice have always left people wondering whether Jephthah actually went ahead and killed his daughter or whether God stopped

When the judge Jephthah returns home victorious, his daughter runs to greet him. He must then sacrifice her as he had promised.

the sacrifice as he did with Isaac in Genesis 22:10–12. Pseudo-Philo leaves no doubt. He first has God affirm that the daughter must die because of her father's foolishness. But the sting of death is eased because she will be gathered to the "bosom of her mothers."

Then, giving her a name, Seila (meaning, "the one requested"), Pseudo-Philo includes a long lament spoken while the girl tearfully wanders Mount Stelac (possibly Mt. Hermon). This song chronicles the things she will never experience: the marriage chamber and the gown and flowers that would mark her as a bride.

When she returns, Jephthah proceeds with a holocaust ritual, placing his daughter as a burnt offering on his altar. Her virgin companions bury her, and four days of mourning are established for Seila each year starting on the 14th day of that month.

Solomon and the Temple

❖ ❖ ❖ ❖

BIBLICAL BACKGROUND

THE STORY OF SOLOMON is told in 1 Kings and reiterated in 1 Chronicles 28–2 Chronicles 9. It emphasizes his wisdom (1 Kings 3:3–28; 4:29–34), his role as the temple-builder (1 Kings 5–6, 8), and finally his apostasy, when he builds shrines for the gods of his foreign wives (1 Kings 11:1–13). The extent of Solomon's fame is demonstrated in the visit of the Queen of Sheba and the business empire he established with the help of the Phoenician King Hiram of Tyre (1 Kings 9:26–10:29).

The origins of the traditional belief that Solomon also possessed the knowledge of magic may come from 1 Kings 5:9–14, which tells of his understanding of the nature of plants and animals. This must have been somewhat embarrassing to official Judaism since there is also a tradition that King Hezekiah suppressed and hid Solomon's books of secret knowledge (Hippolytus, A.D. 160–236). On the other hand, Josephus finds Solomon's ability to expel demons a great benefit for humanity, and he even mentions a man of his own day who employs a magical ring like Solomon's to exorcize a demon.

THE UNTOLD STORY OF SOLOMON

Aside from the rather broad themes mentioned above, the *Testament of Solomon* contains little information that parallels the biblical account. Its apparent concern is to demonstrate how Solomon masters the demons and employs them to construct the temple in

Solomon was visited by other monarchs, such as the Queen of Sheba, who would contribute money toward building the temple.

Jerusalem. However, information garnered from the demons provides a virtual textbook of forces that are responsible for the ills of humanity as well as methods for curing those ills.

The narrative begins with Solomon's concern for a young boy who is wasting away. Solomon had shown him great favor, doubling his wages and his ration of food. Yet, inexplicably, the boy continues to grow thinner every day. When asked about this, he says the demon Ornias comes every evening to steal half of his food and wages and to suck on his right thumb, gradually pulling the very soul out of the boy.

Solomon fervently prays to God for a means of gaining authority over this demon, thus freeing the boy. His prayer is answered when the archangel Michael brings him a seal ring that has the power to imprison demons of every sort. Solomon takes it to the boy and instructs him on how to use the ring to master the demon. Once he is captured, Ornias offers the boy a treasure of gold and silver if he will release him. Not to be tempted or fooled, the boy refuses Ornias' offer and brings him before Solomon.

Once Ornias has been questioned, Solomon calls on the angel Ouriel to aid him in mastering the demon. With this accomplished, the king requires Ornias to take the ring and summon Beelzeboul. The prince of demons thus becomes Solomon's chief source of information on the whole world of these fiends. As Solomon's curiosity is aroused, Beelzeboul is forced to summon one demon after another so that the king may question them.

As Solomon assembles these demons, he asks each his or her name, the sign of the zodiac that each represents, their powers, forms, and the means whereby he or she may be thwarted. Solomon then binds each

SOLOMON'S TESTAMENT

The source for this "untold story" is the *Testament of Solomon*, which was probably written between A.D. 100–400 by a Greek-speaking Christian. Since influences from the folklore and religion of several cultures are evident, the author may have lived in either Egypt, Asia Minor, Syria-Palestine, or Babylonia. Surviving in several medieval manuscripts, this work is a textbook on demonology, angelology, astrology, and magical remedies for disease. Its original purpose may have been as a medical treatise, using Solomon's name to add authority to the writing.

demon to his will with the ring and assigns it a task, usually associated with construction of the temple.

Thus the king learns that Ornias lives in Aquarius, takes on the shape of a winged beast or a lion, especially enjoys the opportunity to attack effeminate boys, and can be stopped by the angel Ouriel. Solomon puts him to work cutting stone blocks for the temple. Similarly, when the female demon Onoskelis appears, she tells Solomon that she lives in Capricorn, travels by the power of the full moon, and works to pervert men from their true natures. While her upper body is in the shape of a beautiful woman, she has the legs of a mule. She may be thwarted by Solomon himself. After acquiring these details, he sets her to spinning hemp for ropes.

Another female demon, Obyzouth, is too dangerous to even be given a task. This Medusa-like creature with "disheveled hair" can only be thwarted from her occupation of killing newborns by the angel Raphael or by having her name written on a piece of papyrus. Solomon orders that she be hung up by her hair in front of the temple. Such a display of power over evil would provide the Israelites further reason to glorify God.

In some cases, especially with the major demons, Solomon also receives predictions of the future. For instance, Enepsigos, a two-headed female demon, prophecies the division of the kingdom as well as the destruction of Jerusalem and the Temple by the Chaldeans. Similarly, when Asmodeus, born of a fallen angel and a human mother, comes bound before Solomon, the demon is extremely arrogant. Resentful at being questioned, he taunts Solomon, telling him that his kingdom will one day be divided and the humans will worship demons as gods since they do not know the names of the angels who thwart them.

After a flogging, Asmodeus declares himself to be the renowned cause of wickedness throughout the world. He claims to cause dissension between newlyweds, madness in women, and countless murders. Despite his anger, the demon is compelled to admit that he can be thwarted by the angel Raphael and also by the liver and gall of catfish smoking on coals, and he may be imprisoned by water. Having drained him of this information, Solomon surrounds Asmodeus with jars of water and smoking fish liver and sets him to work molding clay vessels for the temple.

The questioning of Beelzeboul is also particularly enlightening to the king. Beelzeboul was once the highest-ranking of God's angels, but when he fell he was imprisoned on earth. It is his task to cause destruction by raising tyrants, instigating wars, seducing humans to worship demons, and subverting the piety of priests.

THE DEMONS

The male and female demons described in the *Testament of Solomon* are either fallen angels or the offspring of these angels and human women. They have the ability to change shape and even take on the shining appearance of a god or an angel if they confront a person who does not know the name or symbol needed to thwart their powers. They are associated with stars, but also frequent tombs and desolate places. Beelzeboul is their leader, but they share authority over many places on earth. Their primary purpose is to bring illness, immorality, disaster, and death to humanity.

The demon says that only God himself may thwart Beelzeboul, and he is forced to flee at the speaking of the oath "the Elo-I" ("my God"—spoken by Jesus on the cross in Mark 15:34). Solomon then puts him to work cutting marble in a quarry in Thebes, Egypt. This menial task causes all the other demons to cry out in rage and frustration.

Among the other beings who are brought to Solomon's summons are Lix Tetrax (the demon of the wind), the seven heavenly bodies (Deception, Strife, Fate, Distress, Error, Power, "The Worst"), the headless demon Murder, the dog-shaped demon Scepter, and the three-headed dragon spirit. Each in turn reveals his or her secrets and, in some cases, provides items for the temple treasury. For example, Scepter points the way to an enormous emerald.

The parade of demons seems endless. At one point Solomon is confronted by 36 other "heavenly bodies." Despite their varied shapes, from human to dragons, they at first speak as a chorus when questioned, but then are forced to individually reveal their names and powers. The decans, as they are known, each rule over 10 degrees of the 360 degrees of the astral zodiac. They explain that each of them has been given authority over a different part of the human body. Thus Oropel attacks the throat, Sphandor causes paralysis of the limbs, and Karael is responsible for stomach disorders. As the litany goes on, each bit of data is recorded by Solomon along with the name or charm needed to expel the demon. Solomon explains as part of his *Testament* that he does this so that his sons and their descendants will be able to escape the worst of these evils.

Once this survey of the multitude of demons is complete, the *Testament* turns to the tradition of Solomon's wisdom. This is demonstrated in the biblical text with the story of the two prostitutes who argue over a child (1 Kings 3:16–28). In the *Testament*, Solomon is confronted by one of his artisans, who claims that his son has violently attacked him and now asks the king for justice. When Solomon attempts to sort this out with the son, he is interrupted by Ornias' laughter. The king angrily dismisses the son and demands to know why the demon dares to laugh at him. Ornias explains that he is amused because he knows the father's real intent is to kill his son. Trying to prevent a tragedy, Solomon makes the father swear to bring his son to him in three days unharmed.

Now Solomon turns to Ornias and demands how he could know the son's fate. Ornias explains that the demons regularly fly among the stars to eavesdrop on the decisions God makes regarding humanity. However, they have to pay for their curiosity since there is no way station for them between heaven and earth; their fall back to the lower realm is the explanation for shooting stars.

When the father is summoned back to Solomon's court, he confesses that his son is dead. The king, realizing that Ornias' prediction has come true, can only glorify God who controls all events in heaven and on earth.

Solomon's fame as a wise ruler is further demonstrated by the visits of other monarchs, who marvel and then contribute to the cost and decoration of the temple. Among those who come is Sheba, the Queen of the

South. In the biblical account, the Queen of Sheba comes to test Solomon's wisdom (1 Kings 10:1–15). His willingness to answer any question leads to the development of a strong friendship (1 Kings 10:13) and a huge donation to the Temple fund (120 talents of gold, which is equal to 8,000 pounds).

The *Testament*, however, introduces Sheba as an arrogant witch. She is given a complete tour of the Temple complex and only reluctantly bows to Solomon, acknowledging his wisdom and power. There is no hint of a warm relationship here; her donation of only 10,000 copper shekels is a further indication.

The last step in completing the temple comes when Solomon does a service for the king of Arabia. That monarch is plagued by a wind demon and, having heard of Solomon's wisdom, sends a letter pleading for help.

THE EVIL POWER OF DEMONS

In the cosmology of the *Testament of Solomon*, God is the Lord of heaven and earth. However, the demons "reside" in stars, constellations, the seven planets (moon, sun, Jupiter, Venus, Mercury, Saturn, Mars), and the points of the zodiac. The demons' association with the stars may be based on the previous associations these bodies have in ancient Near Eastern and Greek religions. Evidence of horoscopes, based on the position of the stars and one's date of birth, exists from as early as 400 B.C. The demons are able to use the power of the heavenly bodies to cause madness and physical ills. But their evil power does not go unchecked: Each can be controlled or imprisoned by one of God's angels, and a knowledge of the stars and their properties can serve as the basis for medical treatment by driving away evil when it appears in the form of an illness.

The demons' aim was the corruption and death of humanity.

The message arrives on the same day that Solomon and his artisans are despairing about how to move the temple's huge cornerstone into its proper place. Seeing this plea as an opportunity to complete two tasks at once, Solomon sends a servant with his magic seal ring and instructs him how to capture the wind demon in a leather wine flask.

The imprisoned demon, named Ephippas, is brought back to Solomon for interrogation. When asked how he may be thwarted, the being says, "By the one who is going to be born from a virgin and be crucified by the Jews," a clear reference to Jesus and an indication of Christian influence on the *Testament*. The demon is then instructed to set the cornerstone. The prophet Isaiah metaphorically describes the laying of the cornerstone, but naturally gives God the credit for this task (Isaiah 28:16).

With this stone in place, Solomon rejoices, quoting Psalm 118:22: "The stone rejected by the builders has become the keystone." This passage is also used in the New Testament to refer to the emergence of the new Christian movement (Matthew 21:42–43). Once again, the *Testament* goes beyond its time period to predict events in the Christian era.

SOLOMON'S APOSTASY

Despite his wisdom and many accomplishments, Solomon is also known for the sin of apostasy (turning away from his faith). He allows his foreign wives to worship many gods and even builds them shrines in the vicinity of Yahweh's temple (1 Kings 11:1–13). For this crime, God allows the kingdom to be divided, with the ten northern tribes of Israel forming their own nation under King Jeroboam (1 Kings 12:16–19).

The *Testament of Solomon* draws on this tradition, but focuses it on Solomon's love for a Shummanite woman. When Solomon asks the priests of the Jebusite gods to give this woman to him as his wife, they say he may wed her only if he agrees to worship their gods. This is an interesting parallel to the condition Jacob's sons placed on Shechem, insisting that he be circumcised when he asked to marry their sister Dinah (Genesis 34:13–17). Knowing that it was wrong, but stricken with the woman's beauty, Solomon agrees to sacrifice five locusts to the Jebusite gods Raphan and Molech. When Solomon takes the Shummanite woman back to his palace she convinces him to build temples and worship idols as well.

Now, as he is about to die, Solomon looks back at these sins, and asks his children to pray for him. He urges them not to fall into the same condition themselves, for Solomon had become a laughingstock to the demons. These beings knew the future and could see that they would only be contained a short time, until Solomon fell from grace.

The Prophets of Israel

❖ ❖ ❖ ❖

BIBLICAL BACKGROUND

THE PROPHETS were prominent figures in the history of Israel, connecting the people with the voice of the Lord and calling the people to full, correct observance of the Law of God. They reminded the people of the benefits of remaining loyal to God and the dangerous consequences of serving other gods and ignoring God's commandments. Jews and Christians alike were interested in knowing more about these prophets than could be found in the Old Testament.

Of special interest around the turn of the era were stories about the deaths of the prophets. The Letter to the Hebrews, for example, reflects an awareness of these traditions: "They were stoned to death, they were sawn in two, ... they were killed by the sword" (11:37). Early Christians seized on this tradition to suggest that the murder of the prophets was connected to their witness of the coming Messiah. The last words of Stephen before his own martyrdom bear witness to this linkage: "Which of the prophets did your forebears not persecute? They killed those who had previously announced the coming of the Righteous One" (Acts 7:53).

ELIJAH AND ELISHA

These two figures were very well regarded among the prophets. Their story is found in 1 Kings 17 through 2 Kings 13. It was common in antiquity for traditions to arise about the births of great leaders or other prominent persons, particularly concerning the signs that accompanied their births as omens of their future activities and stature. When the birth of Elijah draws near, his father sees a vision of angelic beings greeting the baby, wrapping the boy in fire, and feeding him flames of fire. The father goes to Jerusalem to learn the meaning of this sign, and he is told that his son will speak words of judgment in Israel and will live in God's light.

The prophet Elijah lives in a cave while he hides from the wicked queen Jezebel.

Elisha was Elijah's disciple and successor, and his birth also produced a tell-tale "sign." King Jeroboam had erected two golden calves in the Northern kingdom of Israel at the two cultic shrines he had set up. These were probably not meant to be idols for worship. Israelites frequently envisioned God's throne as a chariot drawn by strange angelic creatures, or as a chair set upon such creatures. It is likely that Jeroboam's "calves" were meant to represent these beings, signaling the nearness of God's throne. Nevertheless, these images were seen and denounced as idols. When Elisha was born, one of these golden calves bellowed so loudly it was heard in

Jerusalem (about twelve miles away). This was taken as a sign that "a prophet had been born" who would destroy Israel's carved images and idols.

JONAH

Jonah is well known as the prophet who sought to avoid answering God's call by fleeing on a ship bound for Tarshish, but was brought back by a divine detour in the belly of a fish to the shores of Nineveh. There he proclaims that after forty days Nineveh will be destroyed for its idolatry and wickedness. The people of Nineveh repent, so God spares the city. After his "success," Jonah pouts in the desert outside of Nineveh, waiting to see God consume it from heaven. Instead, God chides Jonah for his lack of compassion on a city of people who are precious in God's sight.

Here the legendary expansions take over. After returning home from preaching in Nineveh, Jonah is aware of the potential for being reproached as a false prophet—for Nineveh was not destroyed after forty days as he had said

The prophet Jonah tries to avoid God's call, but is delivered to the shores of Nineveh by a large fish.

100

it would be. This helps to explain his reluctance to go to Nineveh in the first place and his bitterness at the end of the canonical story, after God has spared the foreign city. Jonah knows that God will not destroy the people, but rather will only lead them to repent (Jonah 4:2), and so he knows that his word will be proven false and his reputation ruined. Taking his mother, Jonah leaves his hometown and moves to a Gentile city on the coast of Palestine where he can be anonymous.

Here Jonah's story and Elijah's story come together in Jewish tradition. Elijah curses the land with drought for three years on account of the rampant idolatry in Israel supported by King Ahab and his wife, Jezebel. Elijah flees the king's anger by leaving his jurisdiction, coming to the coastland city where Jonah and his mother live. He stays with them, "for he could not stay with uncircumcised people." The widow's son dies and God raises him back to life through Elijah (see 1 Kings 17). Jonah is identified as that same son. Just as Jonah could not fly from God's presence by going to Tarshish, so he learns that he cannot run from God even in death.

The stories are linked to show that Elijah did not in fact lodge with Gentiles when he stayed in Zarephath (thus violating Jewish purity and kosher laws). First Kings 17 is silent on this matter, and Jesus uses the story of Elijah and the widow to show that God has a special concern for extending his mercy to the Gentiles (see Luke 4:25–26). The author of the *Lives of the Prophets* does not share this universalist outlook, guiding the reader instead to think that Elijah did not give God's benefits to a Gentile woman when Israel was undergoing such hardship.

ISAIAH

The *Lives of the Prophets* includes a short section on Isaiah, but the main source for extrabiblical accounts of this prophet is the *Ascension of Isaiah*. Some scholars hold that this was originally a Jewish work that was expanded by Christian editors. However, it is more likely (given the amount of material that is undoubtedly of Christian origin) that the document was originally written by a Christian living in the first half of the second century A.D.

The tradition about Isaiah's martyrdom at the hands of the wicked king Manasseh was used as the launching point for the author to encourage Christians of his own time. Many were facing, possibly for the first time, persecution from Roman authorities as well as disappointment with church leaders who were more interested in personal power and gain than shepherding their flocks. Christian interest in Isaiah, and in expansions

SOURCES ABOUT THE PROPHETS

The most comprehensive source for these stories is the *Lives of the Prophets*. This book was probably written early in the first century A.D. when there was a resurgence of interest in the graves of the prophets (see Luke 11:47). The collection was written in Greek (the language is often more closely reminiscent of the Septuagint, the Greek translation of the Jewish Scriptures, than the Hebrew texts we know). While it was written by a non-Christian Jew, the collection was preserved by the church with the result that one finds many Christian glosses or additions to the original. The *Lives* are interested in the prophets mainly as miracle workers, intercessors, and diviners.

The faithful, law-abiding prophet Isaiah was also a scholar, advisor, statesman, and poet.

on the biblical account of his life and prophetic ministry, should come as no surprise. Early Christians found the canonical book of Isaiah to be a rich resource for expressing their conviction that Jesus was the Messiah, the agent of God who would bring redemption and restoration for God's people. The *Ascension of Isaiah*, in fact, summarizes Isaiah's prophetic career as an announcement of the saving work of the "Beloved," the Son of God.

This text shows Isaiah leaving his body and taking a tour, conducted by an angel, of the seven heavens. When he at last reaches the seventh and highest heaven, he sees the Son of God and even the Father himself. There he hears God commission the Son to descend through the lower six heavens, disguising himself as a lower angel. This way, none of the lower orders of angels, including Satan (here called Sammael and Beliar) and his hosts who dwell in the space between earth and the lowermost heaven, will recognize him (this is a narrative expansion of 1 Corinthians 2:8). The

Son will take on a human body, be born of a virgin, work great signs and miracles, be crucified by his people at the instigation of Satan, rise from the dead, send out his disciples to convert the nations, and ascend back to his Father's side in his full glory, to the adoration of all the angel hosts.

Isaiah makes his vision known, predicting also the events of the last days. In those days, Beliar (Satan) himself will appear as a man, declare himself to be a god, and establish his cult throughout the empire. The congregation planted by the twelve apostles will suffer persecution from evil rulers—the pawns of Beliar—and will also be eroded from within by self-seeking leaders. Nevertheless, the Beloved will come from heaven, drag Beliar into the pit of fire, judge those who oppress the church, and bring the righteous to their eternal reward.

Because Isaiah exposes Beliar's deception and announces his defeat, Beliar is enraged with Isaiah and works to bring about his death. After the death of the righteous king Hezekiah, his wicked son Manasseh ascends the throne. The devil clings closely to Manasseh, strengthening his efforts to promote apostasy and idolatry in Jerusalem. Isaiah, who had served under Hezekiah, leaves Jerusalem for Bethlehem and, finding the wickedness spread even to that place, removes himself to the desert with a group of loyal prophets. A resident of Bethlehem, named Belkira, discovers Isaiah's hiding place. He goes to Jerusalem and denounces Isaiah and his circle as false prophets who speak lies about the coming destruction of Jerusalem. Isaiah in particular has been taken in a lie, Belkira claims, since Moses said that no one could see God's face and survive, whereas

Isaiah has claimed to have seen God (see Isaiah 6). Manasseh and his courtiers are pleased with Belkira's words and his provision of a pretext for acting against Isaiah. They arrest Isaiah, and Manasseh orders him to be killed by being sawn in two. As the executioners begin to cut through Isaiah's middle, Belkira stands beside him, urging him to retract all his prophecies and give assent to Manasseh's ways. Isaiah instead curses Belkira, whom he recognizes to be Satan, along with all his hosts, and he dies a martyr's death.

JEREMIAH

The prophet Jeremiah was active during the reigns of the last kings of Judah, after Judah became a client kingdom of the Babylonian empire. Jeremiah called for obedience to God's Law as the only path to national safety, rejecting the notion that flawless performance of the Temple cult and God's covenant with David were pillars enough for the survival of the nation. He also advocated submission to the Babylonian overlords, and was proven correct when a rebellion against them brought about the siege of Jerusalem and destruction of the Temple in 587 B.C. After this traumatic event, Jeremiah stayed in his native land to encourage the people who were left there. But after the Babylonian governor was killed by revolutionaries, Jeremiah left for Egypt with many Jewish refugees before the Babylonian forces came to retaliate.

The majority of traditions associated with Jeremiah beyond what can be found in the Old Testament center on his activity in the years (and, frequently, the days) surrounding the destruction of the Temple, his ministry to the exiles thereafter, and his martyrdom at the hands of his fellow Jews.

In a fragment preserved from the historian Eupole-mus (158/7 B.C.), Jeremiah denounces his fellow Jews for their practice of idolatry and announces the coming destruction of Jerusalem. King Jonachim (perhaps Je-

JEREMIAH AND BARUCH

The major sources for traditions about Jeremiah are found in books bearing the name of Jeremiah's secretary, Baruch. For instance, *2 Baruch* is an apocalypse written around A.D. 100 in Hebrew (but surviving only in Syriac) somewhere in Palestine. It was written in Baruch's name, but really wrestles with the much later challenges of recovering God's promises and Jewish hope after the destruction of Jerusalem by the Roman army in A.D. 70. The writings of *2 Baruch* consist mainly of visions and conversations between Baruch and supernatural beings that affirm God's control over history. They also highlight the inevitable fulfillment of God's promises for the righteous and the judgment of the impious. Even while Jews lament the loss of their shepherds (leaders), their light, and their fountains, Baruch informs them that the Torah will be their shepherd, their light, and their fountain. Those who adhere to the Law of Moses will never lack God's guidance and blessing. This apocalypse belongs to that move within Judaism at the end of the first century A.D. to put Torah forward as the sole pillar of Jewish identity.

Another document is *4 Baruch*, also called *Things Omitted from the Book of Jeremiah*. This is a Hebrew work (surviving mainly in Greek, but also in Slavonic, Ethiopic, and Armenian) from the first or second century A.D. It is full of legendary material about Jeremiah, Baruch, and Jeremiah's friend, Abimelech. Written by a Jew but preserved within the church, many Christian additions are also apparent, most notably in the account of Jeremiah's death.

hoiachin is meant) sentences Jeremiah to be burned to death, but Jeremiah says that the wood they are gathering for his pyre will instead be used to dig canals in Babylon and cook food for their Babylonian captors. Word of Jeremiah's prediction comes to the ears of Nebuchadnezzar, the Babylonian king, giving him assurance of a successful campaign to conquer Judea. He joins forces with the ruler of the Medes and sweeps through Palestine, adding it to his kingdom.

Just before Jerusalem is to be taken by the Babylonian army, God warns Jeremiah and his secretary Baruch to leave the

Baruch, Jeremiah's secretary, recorded the prophet's various teachings and prophecies.

city, for their prayers have made the city impregnable. Jeremiah (in *4 Baruch*; it is Baruch who voices this concern in *2 Baruch*) prays that God will not give the idolatrous king a reason to boast that he has captured the city of the living God, and God assures Jeremiah that enemy hands will not overthrow Jerusalem. God shows Jeremiah that angels with torches already stand at the city walls ready to overthrow Jerusalem themselves. Jeremiah receives instructions from God concerning the ark of the covenant, the vestments of Aaron, and the vessels consecrated for use in the Temple, and he hides them in the earth, where they will remain concealed until the last days. This tradition was of remarkable importance for early Judaism, demonstrated by its presence, with some variations, in numerous sources (2 Baruch, 4 Baruch, 2 Maccabees 2:4–8, Lives of the Prophets, and Eupolemus). On the one hand, it suggests that the artifacts that most closely linked the Israelites with God were not defiled by the Gentile invaders, but it also made provision for a future time when God would restore the Temple along with the rest of Jerusalem.

In another tale, found in 4 Baruch, Jeremiah is concerned about the fate of Abimelech, a loyal servant and dear friend for many years (see Jeremiah 38:4–13 for their first encounter). On the morning of the destruction of the city, Jeremiah, wanting to spare Abimelech the sight of Jerusalem in ruins, sends him to a field outside the city to gather figs for the poor. When midday comes, Abimelech, tired from the heat, sleeps. When he awakens 66 years later, both he and the figs are unchanged. Thinking he had enjoyed just a short nap, he returns to the city. Finding everything changed, he supposes he has gotten lost and leaves Jerusalem. Looking for landmarks on the road, he comes once again to Jerusalem and, not finding anyone he knows, sits down by the side of the road completely confused. Through a conversation with an old man, he discovers what has happened to him and to Jerusalem. While he prays, an angel takes him to a tomb where Baruch has gone to lament the fall of the city. Baruch sees in Abimelech an assurance that God will both raise the dead to life and restore Israel to life. They send word to Jeremiah that God is restoring Israel, and Jeremiah (who in *4 Baruch*, was said to have gone into exile in Babylon) prepares the exiles to return.

After bringing back the exiles to Jerusalem and re-joicing with Baruch and Abimelech, Jeremiah falls into a trance for three days. This is the clearest evidence of Christian rewriting of Jeremiah traditions, and shows clear dependence on the *Ascension of Isaiah.* At the end of this three-day period (symbolizing the time that the Messiah would spend in the tomb), Jeremiah rises and prophesies about the coming of the Messiah. The Son of God, Jesus the Christ, will come in the flesh and choose twelve apostles who will proclaim him to the nations. The people become angry saying, "Here is another one who claims, like Isaiah, to have seen God and the Son of God," and they murder Jeremiah by stoning.

The *Lives of the Prophets*, following the biblical account more closely than *4 Baruch*, notes that Jeremiah was taken to Egypt by his fellow Jews, who fled there sometime after the destruction of Jerusalem in 587 B.C. To the biblical account, this collection adds the following anecdote: Jeremiah was held in high esteem by the Egyptians, for at his prayer the asps and crocodiles no longer came near Pharaoh's palace. After his own people stone him (this time in Egypt), the Egyptians bury him near the palace, using the dust over his grave as an antidote to asp bites. Alexander the Great transfers the prophet's remains to Alexandria, where they are buried at different points around the circumference of the city, protecting the whole city from asps and crocodiles.

EZEKIEL

Ezekiel was a priest and prophet active before the destruction of Solomon's Temple by the Babylonians in 587 B.C. and during the first several decades of the captivity of the exiles from Judah in Babylon. The *Lives* reports miracles that Ezekiel accomplished for his fellow Jews during their exile. On one occasion, a large group of pious Jews gathers around Ezekiel by the river Chebar, presumably for worship or to hear Ezekiel's prophecies about the return to Israel. Certain Babylonians, fearing that a revolutionary plot is under way, gather some local troops and set out to break up the gathering. Ezekiel parts the river and allows his congregation to cross. Those Babylonians who pursue them drown as the river returns to its normal course. On another occasion, when many Jews are in danger of starving, Ezekiel supplies them with fish (presumably from the same river) through prayer. These stories are, of course, patterned after God's provision for the Hebrews through Moses at the Red Sea (see Exodus 14) and in the wilderness. The period of exile in Babylon came to be viewed as a second enslavement in a foreign land, and the way back to Israel became a second Exodus.

Ezekiel reproaches the tribes of Dan and Gad for their idolatry and their persecution of the Jews who wish to continue keeping the Law of Moses while in exile. At his pronouncement, snakes arise and devour their infants and flocks. Enraged, the ruler of the Jews in exile, a member of one of the condemned tribes, orders Ezekiel's execution. There are several traditions about the manner of this execution. Some suggest that Ezekiel was beheaded; the Christian *Apocalypse of Paul* and *Acts of Philip* say that he was dragged over the rocks by his feet until he died of head injuries.

DANIEL

Daniel went to Babylon as a captive from Jerusalem in 587 B.C. As a young man he was taken, along with several of his companions, to the court of Nebuchadnezzar, to be groomed for service in the king's court. These young men kept themselves from eating foods not allowed by the Torah (Daniel 1) and stood out because of their intellectual abilities and physical appearance. Daniel especially distinguished himself as an interpreter of dreams (Daniel 2, 4–5) and seer of visions (Daniel 7–12). These men preferred death over disloyalty to God, but God saved them from paying the ultimate price for their faith (Daniel 3, 6).

Several stories about Daniel (composed during the second century B.C.—early enough to be included in the Septuagint translation of Daniel) circulated independently of the version found in the Jewish and Protestant canon of the Old Testament, but are preserved in the Catholic and Orthodox canons (what Protestants refer to as the "Apocrypha"). The first of these stories, set within the Jewish community living in Babylon after the conquest of Jerusalem, shows Daniel's astounding insight while still a young lad. A rich and honored Jew named Joakim marries an exceedingly beautiful girl named Susanna, who is diligent in obeying God's Torah. Because of his spacious accommodations and his standing in the community, Joakim's house serves as a meeting place for Jews in exile, in particular as a council chamber where the elders could gather.

Two elders are newly appointed and, coming to Joakim's house, catch sight of Susanna and desire to have relations with her. Susanna habitually walked in Joakim's walled garden and bathed in the pool at noon, after the council had broken up. Many weeks pass, until the two elders can stand to suppress their lust no longer. One day, when the council is dismissed, they say their parting greeting and leave with the assembly, but then both come back to the garden and, discovering each other there, confess their mutual passion and agree to look for an opportunity to enjoy the object of their desire. Their chance comes when Susanna, bathing in the pool, sends her maids out to get some olive oil and ointments, bidding them close the door to the garden behind them. The elders leap out from their hiding places and give her an ultimatum: If she will not consent to lie with them, they will accuse her of committing fornication in the garden with a young man. Susanna chooses to embrace danger from human beings rather than sin against God, and she flees from the garden. The elders denounce her as an adulteress, claiming that they tried to restrain the young man but, because he was stronger, they were unable to detain him. The court believes their testimony, since they are elders and judges, and sentences Susanna to die according to the Law of Moses.

As Susanna cries out to God at this act of injustice, God summons the young Daniel to the scene. Daniel chides the assembly for being taken in so easily by these two renegades and proceeds to examine the men separately. "Under which tree," he asks the first elder,

"did you see Susanna and the young man embracing?"
He replies that it was under a mastic tree. Daniel sends
him away and summons the second elder, asking the
same question. This one replies that the couple em-
braced under an evergreen oak. The discrepancy in their
testimony demonstrates to the assembly that they had
borne false witness against Susanna, and so they are
executed instead. From that day on, Daniel enjoyed a
great reputation among his people.

The second story is set late in Daniel's life—after
Nebuchadnezzar, Belshazzar, and Darius have all passed
away and Cyrus, king of Persia, has taken Babylon for
his empire. Cyrus asks Daniel why he avoids the worship of Bel, a chief deity in Babylon. Daniel replies that
he serves the one, true, living God, and that he will not
worship idols made by human hands. Cyrus protests
that Bel is a living god, for every night priests set out
food and drink before Bel's statue, and every morning
the food is gone. Daniel tells the king not to be deceived, for Bel never eats anything. Cyrus angrily questions the priests about this, and tells them to prove that
Bel is a living god or die themselves. The priests invite
the king to set out the food himself, lock the doors of
the temple, and seal the doors with his own signet ring.
The priests leave the temple and Cyrus does as they
suggest. Daniel, ever wise to pagan tricks, orders the
king's servants to sprinkle ashes on the floor of the
temple. In the morning, the king and Daniel return to
find the seal intact. Opening the doors, they find the
food gone. Cyrus gives praise to Bel, but Daniel laughs
and points to the floor where the footprints of the
priests, their wives, and their children are clearly visi-

ble. The priests and their families, forced to reveal the secret door under the altar by which they entered, are executed by the king, and Daniel destroys Bel's statue and temple.

This story continues with a second attempt by Cyrus to get Daniel to acknowledge a pagan deity. Cyrus takes Daniel to see a large reptile (a "dragon") that is worshipped by the Babylonians as a living god. Daniel refuses to worship the dragon, but asks permission of the king to kill it using neither sword nor club. Daniel makes cakes out of boiled pitch, fat, and hair, and feeds these to the dragon, whose bowels burst open at once. The local leaders of the Babylonians are enraged. Blaming the king for the destruction of both their beloved gods, they threaten to revolt and kill him unless he delivers Daniel over to them. These leaders throw Daniel into the lions' den (now the second time for this man) and leave him there for seven days, but he is once again miraculously preserved by the God he has so faithfully served. Cyrus, delighted to find Daniel in one piece, has him pulled out and then casts his accusers to the lions, who promptly devour them.

This second story celebrates the powerlessness of pagan gods and the superiority of the God of Israel, the "living God who created heaven and earth." Surrounded and vastly outnumbered by the worshippers of other gods, Jews needed frequent reminders that they alone were the ones in touch with divine realities. Such stories helped Jews, particularly in the Diaspora (Jewish communities outside of Palestine), remain loyal to their ancestral religion and resist the pressure to assimilate to the ways of the pagan majority.

Esther

BIBLICAL BACKGROUND

THERE ARE TWO BOOKS in the Old Testament named after women: Esther and Ruth. Some Hellenistic Jews had problems with the story of Esther. The Hebrew version contains no mention of God or of prayer for divine intervention. In addition, having a female as the main character may have slowed the acceptance of this book into the official canon. The Additions to Esther, therefore, were added to deal with some of these theological and social concerns. This Greek version greatly increased God's role in the narrative and also gave Mordecai a much more significant position. The vengeance factor, so prominent in Esther 9:5, is also softened, and the number of enemies slain is drastically reduced (75,000 in Esther 9:16 compared to 15,000 in the Greek version). The Apocryphal Additions to Esther are embedded throughout the canonical book, providing information and clarification of the narrative details (including copies of the king's letters and a description of Mordecai's dream).

THE ADDITIONS TO ESTHER

The biblical version of the story of Esther begins with a magnificent banquet held by the Persian king, Ahasuerus (also known as Xerxes). However, the author(s) of the Additions to Esther wanted to enhance Mordecai's place in the story. Therefore they begin when Mordecai, a Jew serving at the Persian court of Artaxerxes (Xerxes) at Susa, has a frightening dream on

Esther approaches King Ahasuerus without being summoned and is so frightened by his increasing rage that she faints in front of him.

New Year's Day. He sees two dragons preparing to engage in combat and many nations equipping themselves for war against a "righteous nation." The people of this nation cry out to God for assistance, and they are answered by the appearance of a mighty river, the reemergence of the sun from the gloom that had existed, and the exalting of the lowly. Knowing this is a sign of things to come, Mordecai dwells thoughtfully on this divine message.

That same day, as Mordecai sits in his usual place in the palace courtyard, he overhears a conversation between two of the king's eunuchs who are plotting to assassinate Artaxerxes. Mordecai immediately reports this threat to the king's life. Since he was required to file a formal report of the events, Mordecai may have actually been a member of the king's "secret service." In any case, because of his action, Mordecai is given a higher place at court and rewarded. His rise to prominence, however, is threatened by another of the king's advisors, Haman. He is the villain of this tale. Even his name "the Agagite" (*Bougaean* in Greek) lets the audience know he will work to destroy Mordecai and the Jews. This is based on the fact that Agag was a king of the Amalekites (1 Samuel 15:32), the longtime enemies of the Jewish people.

When the biblical story begins, the extravagant king is throwing a 180-day party to demonstrate his great wealth and power. He attempts to top off the celebrations by asking Queen Vashti to come out and display her beauty to his drunken guests. She refuses to demean herself, but this puts both her and the king in a difficult position, since no one in ancient Persia could deny the king. Naturally, Xerxes is outraged and asks his advisors what to do. The advisors tell the king that if he allows Vashti to get away with this defiance, then every wife in the kingdom will use it as an excuse to refuse their husbands' commands. The result is that Vashti is "demoted." She loses her position as queen and, like King David's wife Michal (see 2 Samuel 6:21–23), she is relegated to the loneliness of the harem chambers for the rest of her life.

To replace Vashti, the royal court stages a beauty contest to find another queen. This is where Esther enters the story. Esther, like all the other "eligible females" of the kingdom, is gathered up in the royal draft and undergoes an elaborate cosmetic regime for a full year. She charms everyone she meets and, after winning the king's favor, is crowned queen.

The secret in the story, however, is that Esther is a Jew. At this point, both the biblical story and the Additions increasingly revolve around this element in connection with a plot against the Jewish people throughout the Persian empire. Esther had been raised by her cousin (or uncle in some translations) Mordecai, the man who had won the king's favor. He is given the honor of sitting at the gate to the palace, a prominent place and one from which he could both conduct business and learn the secrets that swirl around a royal court.

Conflict now begins when Mordecai, sitting at the gate of the palace, refuses to bow to Haman, the king's adviser (Esther 3:2). This publicly humiliates a very vain man, and Haman hatches a scheme to gain a terrible revenge. He is able to convince the king that the Jews are a dangerous element within the Persian empire and must be exterminated (Esther 3:8–13). Duped into believing this lie, Xerxes issues a decree that on a certain date all of the Jews within the empire are to be killed.

Eventually Mordecai, who hears the whisperings of the city from his seat at the gate, learns of the plot. The biblical version has him leave the gate area and go to Queen Esther. He coolly tells her of the coming danger and reminds her that she must take the side of Jews, if only to save her own life (Esther 4:13–16). If she doesn't take action, her secret will ultimately be revealed, and she will die with all the rest. But if she can summon the courage, she has a chance to save them all.

The author of the Additions, perhaps reacting to the lack of any mention of God at this desperate moment, has Mordecai pray at this point in the narrative. He calls on the Lord, the ruler of heaven and earth, to hear him. Mordecai declares that he had not refused to bow down to Haman out of personal pride: "I would have been willing to kiss the soles of his feet to save Israel." Rather he wished to show this reverence to God alone. Now he beseeches God to spare his people and to "turn their mourning into feasting."

The scene now shifts to Esther who is struggling with this dilemma. The biblical narrative describes how she concocts a plan that will, in her own way, give her the opportunity to reveal to King Xerxes that she is a Jew. If Esther times it correctly, her revelation and the king's desire to save her may save all of the other Jews as well. Again dissatisfied with the idea of a purely human strategy, the Additions inject Esther's prayer at this point. She first clothes herself as a mourner, with ashes and dung in her hair. Then, properly humbled, she cries out to God to save his "inheritance Israel" as he had done in times past.

The author of the Additions may have been scandalized by the very idea that a Jewish women would submit to become the wife of a Gentile. Thus, in this version, Esther declares that although she has been forced to share the bed of the Persian king she has never experienced any pleasure in doing so. Having declared her faith in God's abilities to save them, Esther asks that Haman's plot be foiled and that she be given courage to face this new trial.

Esther sets her plan in motion by taking a risk. According to the traditions of the Persian court, no one is allowed to speak to the king or appear in his presence without his permission. Risking possible execution, Esther arrays herself in her finest robes and stands in the outer court of the palace along with her serving maid. In the biblical version, when the king sees her, he is once again stricken by her beauty and points his scepter towards her—indicating that she may approach him and speak.

The Additions, however, again introduce divine intervention into the story. In this version, the king is livid with anger at seeing Esther standing before him unsummoned. Esther is so frightened by his rising rage that she faints. God then changes the king's anger into concern—he leaps from his throne and gathers her in his arms. He reassures Esther that she will not be executed, for the law applies only to the people, and not to the royal family. He then raises his scepter, allowing her to speak. Esther explains she had been overcome by the splendor of the king's majesty, and then she faints down again.

Having gained the king's attention and sympathy, and perhaps bolstered by the prayers of all the Jews (Esther 4:16), Esther invites Xerxes and his trusted adviser Haman to a banquet in her apartments. The idea appeals to the king, and he is so delighted by her abilities as a hostess that he offers to give her "up to half of the kingdom" (Esther 5:6). However, she does not ask for anything at that first banquet other than a second night of their company.

Thus, Haman and the king go in to feast with Queen Esther for a second day. In the midst of their merrymaking, the king once again tells Esther to ask whatever she wishes of him. At last Queen Esther has the opportunity she has been waiting for, and she uses all of her skills to win the king to her cause, warning him that he has been fooled into ordering the execution of Esther and all of her people.

Xerxes, realizing he has been tricked, asks Esther to name the man who has presumed to do this. With real delight, Esther gestures dramatically and says, "A foe and enemy, this wicked Haman right here." Xerxes orders the guards to arrest him and have him hung from the 72-foot-high gallows that Haman had built for Mordecai's execution.

But this does not end the drama. The Additions contain a copy of the decree, written by Mordecai and issued by the king, that reviles Haman for his plotting and frees the Jews to live according to their own laws. But according to Persian law, the king's original decree could not be rescinded. So on the 13th day of Adar, the day before the mass genocide of the Jews was originally to take place, Esther and Mordecai convince Xerxes to give the Jews the right to defend themselves; they proceed to kill many thousands of their enemies (Esther 8:9–12). That day was to become known as Purim and would thereafter be a feast day, fulfilling Mordecai's prayer.

The final segment of the Additions to Esther includes Mordecai's interpretation of his original dream of the two dragons. He now knows that they were himself and Haman. The enemy nations were the provinces of the empire who had been instructed to destroy the "righteous nation" of Israel. The people are thus to celebrate God's deliverance of his people each year on this date, and they have done so ever since.

TOBIT

❖ ❖ ❖

HISTORICAL BACKGROUND

THE KINGDOM ruled by David was divided into two separate nations after the death of his son Solomon in about 930 B.C. The northern ten tribes formed the Kingdom of Israel, while the tribes of Judah and Benjamin became the Kingdom of Judah. Although both kingdoms still considered themselves part of the covenantal community established by God with Abraham and again with Moses, their political and economic policies differed widely. Because the northern kingdom of Israel was better situated geographically and had more fertile agricultural areas, it prospered, while Judah remained an economic backwater. This prosperity, however, had a price. When Assyria began to emerge as the next great nation, Israel was quickly absorbed as

THE BOOK OF TOBIT

The book of Tobit is a **novella** (a literary form shorter than the novel, with a compact style and plot) that deals with the problems of ordinary people. Although it is set in the Exile—specifically during the period immediately after the Israelites were deported by the Assyrians in 721 B.C.— this work was most likely written sometime in the second century B.C. in Greek. The book contains several literary types in addition to the narrative: wisdom admonitions (Tobit 4:5–19), laments (Tobit 3:1–6, 11–15), and prayers of thanksgiving (Tobit 11:14–15; 13:1–17).

a subject state and forced to pay tribute and supply soldiers for Assyria's continuous military campaigns.

Many of the smaller nations in Syria and Palestine resented Assyrian control and the drain on their resources. Whenever an opportunity arose—at the death of an Assyrian king and during the transition of leadership, for instance—they would combine their efforts and revolt. After a series of these revolts, the Assyrian kings Shalmaneser V and Sargon II decided to use extreme measures to solve the problem. Their armies ravaged the entire area in 723–722 B.C., massacring whole city populations and deporting large numbers of people. These exiles were resettled in far-flung areas of the Assyrian empire. The northern kingdom of Israel ceased to exist. Most of its people had been deported, and it is upon this experience that the traditions of the "Ten Lost Tribes of Israel" are founded.

For more than a century after the Assyrian conquest, the prophets of the surviving nation of Judah continued to speak of the lost tribes, but these exiles were never to return. The book of Tobit is one of the few pieces of Hellenistic Jewish literature that is set in the period of the Assyrian exile. The people of the northern tribes, who seem to simply vanish from history after 721 B.C., come alive in this story.

THE TRIALS OF TOBIT

The story of Tobit describes the trials of a devout Jew, much like Job, who suffers for upholding the traditions of his people, and who is eventually rewarded by God for his devotion. One of the major questions raised by the destruction of the northern kingdom was whether God had abandoned the people because of their sinfulness. In particular, when the kings of Israel constructed shrines at Dan and Bethel (1 Kings 12:25–33) and encouraged their people to worship there rather than in Jerusalem, the prophets declared this a violation of the covenant and just cause for God's wrath. This may well explain why Tobit, now living in Nineveh, the Assyrian capital, introduces himself by saying that he had always gone to worship in the Jerusalem temple, unlike most other people of the northern kingdom.

After being taken captive by Shalmaneser V's army, Tobit continues to worship God, even in the midst of the Exile. He carefully observes the laws of his people even though so many others have abandoned them. Tobit is meticulous in keeping the dietary laws and the regulations of ritual purity. He gives alms to the poor and, when the Assyrian government begins a policy of exposing the corpses of dead Jewish prisoners, Tobit secretly retrieves the bodies and gives them proper burial. His devoutness and diligence are rewarded when he is appointed the king's purchasing agent.

Troubles begin, however, when Sennacherib comes to the Assyrian throne. The new king declares it illegal to bury those Jews who had been executed as enemies of the Assyrian state. Since Tobit, out of piety, continues to commit this illegal action, the authorities seize his property and leave him and his family destitute. This is actually the first of several folklore elements in the story, having its origin in a folktale of "The Grateful Dead," about spirits of the dead who reward the living for giving them burial.

Tobit and the other Jews in exile are briefly given hope when Sennacherib is murdered by his sons, and his

When Sennacherib rises to the Assyrian throne, he makes it illegal to bury Jews who are executed as enemies of the state.

successor, Esarhaddon, appoints Tobit's nephew Ahiqar as his finance minister. Ahiqar intercedes for his uncle, and Tobit is restored to his position. But their happiness is short-lived because of Tobit's stubborn piety. On the day of Pentecost (the Jewish Feast of Weeks), Tobit sends his son Tobias into the streets to invite a stranger to share their meal. Tobias discovers another Jewish corpse lying in the street and Tobit insists on rushing out and giving the man burial.

Without a child of his own to be his heir, Ahiqar adopts his sister's son Nadin and trains him to take over his job in the Assyrian court. Once Nadin gets into office, however, he betrays Ahiqar by accusing him of treason. Ahiqar is sentenced to death, but the executioner carries out the sentence on a substitute, and Ahiqar goes into hiding. Ahiqar subsequently recovers his honor by helping the king of Assyria win an enormous wager with the Pharaoh of Egypt and by exposing Nadin as a fool.

Having defiled himself by contact with the dead, Tobit believes he cannot reenter his house until the following day. Thus he stays in a courtyard, and during the night bird droppings strike his eyes and blind him. Because Tobit is now disabled, the family is again without an income. They are briefly supported by Ahiqar, but when they move to Elymais, Tobit faces the humiliation of having to depend on what little money his wife can earn. His frustration is evident when he begins to quarrel with her and she snaps back that his extreme piety and attention to the law have done them no good. Sad and despondent, Tobit prays to God to end his life.

The scene then shifts to another unhappy Jewish family. Raguel and his daughter Sarah live in exile in Ecbatana, the capital of the Median empire. Although a marriage contract has been arranged for Sarah on seven occasions, she remains a virgin. Each time, on her wedding night, the demon Asmodeus appears and kills her bridegroom. This is one of the attributes of Asmodeus revealed to Solomon in the *Testament of Solomon* (see pages 88–97), but Sarah and her father lack the knowledge given to Solomon to thwart the demon. Without a marriage for their daughter to insure care for Raguel and his wife, Edna, in their old age, the older couple faces a grim future. In addition, if there is no heir to inherit the family property, the household will be shamed and their name will become extinct. As a result, on the same night that Tobit prays to God for an end to his suffering, Sarah also prays to die. God hears the pleas of these two desperate people and dispatches the angel Raphael to aid them both. By drawing the two families together, God will provide the solution to their individual problems.

On the same day that Tobit and Sarah lift up their prayers, Tobit prepares for death by admonishing his son to proper behavior. He makes Tobias swear that he will treat his mother with the respect that is due her, "marry a woman from among the descendants of your ancestors," always show concern for the poor and less fortunate, and show reverence to the righteous dead—even pouring wine on their graves.

After giving his son what he believes will be his last words of instruction, Tobit tells Tobias about a sum of money that he has left in trust with a man named Gabael in the Median city of Rages. Once this money is retrieved, the family will be able to survive. However, Tobias does not know the way to Rages and so he must first seek out a guide. He meets an old man named Azarias, who is actually the angel Raphael in disguise. The "old man" assures Tobias that he will successfully lead him to Gabael and even predicts that Tobit will soon be cured of his blindness. A fee of a drachma a day is negotiated, and a bonus is proposed once the journey is completed.

Tobit's wife, Anna, is distressed that her husband is sending their only son on a long and dangerous journey. She bitterly argues against depriving her of the boy. In a wonderful moment of irony, Tobit soothes her by saying that "a good angel" will undoubtedly guide Tobias and protect him throughout the trip.

Along the way, the two men and Tobias's dog make camp beside the Tigris River. Tobias casts out a line hoping to catch a fish for their supper. He is surprised when he finds himself attacked by a monstrous fish that nearly swallows him. When the fish is brought to shore, Azarias (Raphael) instructs him to gut the fish and save its heart, liver, and gall. No explanations are given about this at first, but Tobias soon learns from his guide how these items can be put to use in exorcizing a demon and restoring sight (see the *Testament of Solomon* and the king's interrogation of Asmodeus, pages 88–97).

As they draw near to the city of Ecbatana, Azarias (Raphael) tells Tobias they will lodge with Raguel, a relative of Tobit. He then describes Raguel's beautiful daughter, and suggests that Tobias marry Sarah, thereby fulfilling his father's wish that he marry within the tribe. He also describes this marriage as an obligation since Tobias is the nearest male kin (compare to Genesis 38 and Deuteronomy 25:5–10). However, Tobias has heard about Sarah's marital misfortunes and is not sure he wants to be Asmodeus's eighth victim. He is also concerned that his death would leave his parents without any means of support as they grew older.

Azarias then draws him close and tells him the secret of how to overcome the demon. He first must use the heart and liver of the fish that he had caught to smoke Asmodeus out of the bridal chamber. Then, crying out to God in prayer, the couple will be delivered from any harm. Confident that he will succeed, Tobias enters Raguel's house and falls instantly in love with Sarah.

Naturally, Raguel is pleased to have such a fine young man as a prospective son-in-law. However, moral obligation requires him to warn Tobias about the fate of Sarah's previous bridegrooms. When Tobias assures him he is willing to take the chance, a formal marriage contract is drawn up and preparations are made for the wedding. Fearing what is to come, however, Sarah and her mother weep as they dress her in her wedding gown, and Raguel has his servants secretly prepare a grave for Tobias's body.

But Tobias does not plan to die. As the newly married couple enters their bridal chamber, Tobias places the fish heart and liver on a brazier. The resulting pungent smoke performs its wonder and drives Asmodeus all the way to Egypt to escape its effects. Tobias and Sarah then pray together for God to bless their marriage and to give them the wisdom to recognize that marriage is best when it is based on love and the friendship of the partners. Raguel also praises God and quickly orders that the newly opened grave be immediately filled.

The happy couple remains with Raguel for 14 days, and they receive half of Raguel's wealth as a marriage present. Tobias asks Raphael to visit Rages for him and collect the money from his father's friend Gabael. All this time away from home, however, causes Tobit to become more and more apprehensive about his son's safety. Anna, afraid her son has been killed, goes out everyday to look longingly down the road to the south.

After the 14-day wedding feast, Sarah's parents bless the couple. Accompanied by slaves and animals given to them as part of their marriage contract, Tobias and Sarah set out for Nineveh. As they approach the outskirts of the city, Tobias, his dog, and Raphael hurry up the road where they find Anna. She is nearly overcome with joy, and her cries attract blind Tobit to the scene. Because of his disability, Tobit stumbles coming out of the door, and Tobias rushes up to help him. Then, as instructed by Raphael, Tobias applies a salve made from the fish's gall to his father's eyes. Immediately, the old man regains his sight. The family is restored at last, with Ahiqar joining them for an additional seven days of feasting and rejoicing.

Once the celebration ends, Tobias turns to his son and says they must pay Raphael his wages, plus a bonus. Tobias offers to give him half of what he has obtained in his journey to Media, but the angel tells them to give all the glory to God for what has happened. He instructs them on the proper lifestyle of a law-abiding worshiper of God: prayer accompanied by fasting, almsgiving, and righteous behavior. Raphael's praise of charitable acts and almsgiving justifies Tobit's actions and provides

As instructed by the angel Raphael, Tobias applies a salve made from fish's gall to his father's eyes, and Tobit regains his sight.

reassurance to the reader that good deeds will eventually be rewarded by God.

Raphael then reveals his true nature as one of the seven holy angels of God whose task it is to present the prayers and petitions of saints to the "Holy One." They are afraid and throw themselves to the ground, a typical reaction to the presence of a supernatural being (see Revelation 19:10). He reassures them that no harm will come to them and, after his miraculous disappearance, the family proclaims to all the "wonderful works of God."

The angel had told Tobit to write down all that had occurred so that others would learn of it and praise God, since it is good to "gloriously reveal the works of God." The result is a hymn of thanksgiving that praises God as just: He rewards the righteous and punishes the wicked. There is also a statement of assurance that God will eventually draw all of the scattered tribes of Israel back together in a restored Jerusalem, whose "streets will be paved with beryl and ruby and the stones of Ophir."

The story ends with Tobit's family gathered around his deathbed. Tobit urges them to remain upright and to continue his practice of almsgiving. He also warns them to move from Nineveh to Media. As a good son should, Tobias follows his father's advice. After his mother, Anna, dies, Tobias and Sarah move to Ecbatana and care for Sarah's parents until their deaths. The inheritance they receive from her parents assures the survival and prosperity of the family. Tobias gains some satisfaction at the end of his long life when he hears of the fall of Nineveh at the hands of the Median king Cyaxares. He must have smiled as he saw Assyrian prisoners paraded through the streets of Ecbatana.

Judith

HISTORICAL BACKGROUND

A RECURRENT STORY found in the literature of several ancient Near Eastern cultures describes how a brave woman saved her household's honor and/or her people by lulling an enemy into a false sense of security and then murdering him. The earliest example comes from the north Syrian port city of Ugarit about 1600 B.C. In this case, a woman named Paghat avenges the murder of her brother Aqhat by disguising herself as a barmaid, helping her enemy to drink himself into a stupor, and then killing him with the sword she has concealed under her skirts. The first biblical version of this story is found in Judges 4–5. There the Kenite woman Jael invites the Amorite general Sisera into her tent as he flees from a lost battle with the Israelites. She provides him with a cup of warm milk, a blanket, and a promise to serve as his lookout. Once Sisera falls asleep, secure in the thought that he can have his way with the woman when he is rested, Jael takes a tent peg and drives it so hard through Sisera's temple that it embeds itself into the ground.

During the Hellenistic period (second century B.C.), the Jews were beset with enemies from the Seleucid kingdom, based in Syria. King Antiochus IV issued a series of decrees designed to strip the Jews of what wealth they may have had as well as their cultural heritage. He wished to eliminate the worship of Yahweh (the Hebrew God) and was willing to use force if necessary. The story of Judith represents one of several pieces of literature produced during this time (the book of Daniel is another good example) that attempted to demonstrate to the Jewish people that they could save themselves, with God's help, from even the most vicious of enemies. In this case, Judith plays the same role as Paghat and Jael, tempting the commander of a besieging army and ultimately destroying him.

JUDITH THE FAITHFUL WIDOW

The story of Judith opens against the backdrop of a military and political struggle within the "Assyrian" empire. This struggle begins in Persia and eventually spreads as far as the unknown Israelite town of Bethulia. Nebuchadnezzar, known to history as the great king of the Babylonian empire, is here described as the Assyrian monarch, ruling from the capital at Nineveh. This is the first of many historical confusions in this story and may in fact be a part of the fanciful and comic nature of a story that "mixes and matches" villains from Israel's past. When the Medes refuse to submit to Nebuchadnezzar's rule, a six-year war ensues that will inflame nearly the entire Near East.

The huge Assyrian army (120,000 infantry and 12,000 cavalry, plus support personnel) is commanded by General Holofernes. He successfully cuts his way through Media, Cilicia, and the coastal cities of Syria and Phoenicia, butchering whole populations and forcing rulers to pay tribute and give the king tokens of "earth and water" as the sign of their abject surrender. Everywhere he goes, Holofernes demands that the subject peoples worship Nebuchadnezzar as the "one true god." The itinerary of the campaign gives unrealistic figures for travel (3 days to move 300 miles) and hops all over the map, another sign of the story's fictitious nature.

Realizing that their territory would soon be invaded by the Assyrians, the Israelites fortify their cities. In addition, the high priest of the Jerusalem Temple, Joakim, orders residents from Bethulia and Bethomesthaim to guard a narrow pass that leads to Jerusalem. Such a pass does not actually exist, but was introduced into the story to give Bethulia greater importance.

The Israelites also take the extraordinary step of putting on sackcloth, fasting, and praying to God for their deliverance and for the survival of the Jerusalem Temple. Every man, woman, and child does this, and even the animals are said to be wearing mourning gar-

THE BOOK OF JUDITH

This short story presents itself as a work of fiction from the beginning, as it opens with a series of obvious historical blunders (such as naming Nebuchadnezzar as the king of the Assyrians when he was actually king of the Babylonians). It was written near the end of the second century B.C. The author's familiarity with Palestinian Jewish customs, together with his interest in dietary and purity laws, suggests that he may have been a member of the Pharisaic party. The original language of the book was Hebrew, but the Greek version found in the Septuagint is what has survived. Its story focuses on an event that is described by using a combination of historical and non-historical details in order to highlight the heroic actions of Judith, a Jewish widow. She is portrayed in glowing terms as a pious and upright widow (Judith 8:4–8), who is quite capable of coolly beheading the enemy of her people in order to save them from destruction.

ments. While other biblical references are made to the act of mourning, only in the book of Jonah (3:6–9) are such universal expressions of humble worship made, though in that book it is the Assyrian people and animals of Nineveh who are wearing sackcloth.

Holofernes is mystified by such resistance since he has easily cut a bloody swath through every other country. He consults Achior, the leader of the Ammonites, about this and is given a lesson in Israelite history. Achior recites the saving events of Yahweh, including the exodus, the crossing of the Red Sea, and the conquest of Canaan. However, he says, the Israelites were forced into exile because of their disobedience to their God and have just recently returned to their land and rebuilt their destroyed temple. Achior declares that they can only be defeated in battle if they are currently violating their covenant with God.

Such advice is definitely not what Holofernes wants to hear. The Assyrian general defiantly proclaims that Achior's "prophecies" are false, for "who is God except Nebuchadnezzar?" In his anger, Holofernes orders that Achior be expelled from the camp and sent to die with the Israelites. His servants arrest Achior, bind his hands and feet, and leave him outside the city of Bethulia. Achior is taken in by the people of Bethulia and, after telling them of his experience with the Assyrians, he is lodged with Uzziah, their chief magistrate.

Despite the Israelites' continuous prayers, the Assyrians continue to advance. Taking the advice of the Edomites and Moabites (historic antagonists of the Israelite nation), Holofernes cuts off the city's water supply and waits for their surrender. After 34 days, the people of Bethulia find themselves in dire straits and are amazed that God has not responded to their plight.

Faced with the traditional question of "who truly is God?," the besieged people of Bethulia are about to surrender and bow down to the self-proclaimed divine-king Nebuchadnezzar. The magistrates gather to discuss the situation and, under pressure from the people, they decide to give God only five more days. If God has not raised the siege and saved them by then, they will surrender to the Assyrians.

Here Judith, a chaste and pious widow, enters the story. Displeased with the elders' decision, she lectures them about putting God to the test. God, she says, will do only what he wishes to do and cannot be coerced by human demands. Since the elders cannot come up with a better plan, Judith volunteers to take her maid and go out to the Assyrians. She says that within five days God will deliver the Israelites from their enemies "by her hand" (compare Deborah's prophecy in Judges 4:9).

THE HIDDEN LANGUAGE OF CLOTHING

Clothing is a status marker in the ancient Near East. Its design, weave, and color signify rank and wealth. When a character in the Bible changes clothing, it is often to transform his or her person. Thus when Tamar (and Judith in this story) takes off her widow's garments in Genesis 38:14, she masks her social status and presents herself in a different, more sexually desirable light. Similarly, when David casts aside his robes and dances before the ark of the covenant in only a loincloth in 2 Samuel 6:14, he has stripped away his rank as king and humbled himself as simply one of many Israelite worshipers that day.

Before she goes, Judith once again puts on sackcloth, scatters ashes in her hair, and prays to God for the strength to face this ordeal and for the guile to trick the enemy into making a fatal mistake.

The next day Judith prepares herself for battle. She packs a hamper with enough kosher food for five days. Then she removes her widow's garments and transforms herself into a very desirable woman. She bathes and perfumes her body and puts on fresh makeup and an enticing gown. Every man who sees her as she passes out of the city is overcome with her beauty, which is exactly what she is counting on. An Assyrian patrol takes Judith and her maid into custody almost immediately, but they are overwhelmed by her confident manner and grace and take her directly to Holofernes.

Holofernes is also blind to any danger Judith may represent. He believes she has been captivated by his power and charm and is flattered by her assurance that he will soon see that "God will accomplish something through you." Judith pretends to be the perfect informer. She tells Holofernes all that has transpired within the city and what Achior had told them. Then she reaffirms Achior's prediction that the city will only fall if the people sin against God's law. And, she tells him, they are about to do just that. The siege has nearly exhausted the food supply and now the people are planning to consume the "first fruits of the grain and the tithes of the wine and oil," items that violate the law and would defile them. For this illegal act, Judith continues, God will shortly give the city into Assyrian hands, and she will inform Holofernes the moment that God tells her of the people's violation.

Judith continually refuses to share a meal with Holofernes, preferring to eat the kosher provisions she has brought with her. This only heightens his desire for her. For three days she goes out to pray and then returns to eat her single meal. On the fourth day, Holofernes can stand it no longer. Judith has put him in a state in which he will consent to almost anything to get her within his tent. When he sends his eunuch Bagoas to invite her yet again, she at last agrees to come to a private banquet, saying, "Who am I to refuse my lord?"

As they recline together at their meal, Judith continues to act submissive, agreeing to his invitation to eat and drink freely. She says repeatedly that this will be a night to remember. Holofernes is so pleased by the course of events that he fails to monitor his own drinking and, instead of getting Judith drunk, he consumes

LAWS REGARDING FOOD

The laws of ritual purity, or *kashrut*, restrict Israelite contact with the diseased or those who are impure, such as menstruating women. Certain foods are set aside for God, such as the first fruits of the harvest and the tithe, and they must not be consumed by humans (Exodus 23:19a; Leviticus 27:30). The law also requires that Israelites not mix milk and meat products in the same meal (Exodus 23:19b) and that they eat only certain designated foods and abstain from all others (Leviticus 11). Kosher foods include any animal that has "divided hoofs and is cleft-footed and chews the cud." This would exclude the camel, rock badger, the hare, and the pig. All fish with fins and scales are kosher, but shellfish are forbidden, as are birds of prey and most insects other than locusts and grasshoppers.

After dining with Holofernes, the general of the Assyrian army, Judith cuts off his head and escapes with her maidservant.

"more than he had ever drunk in any one day" and falls into a stupor. Left alone as the servants retire, Judith prays for God to strengthen her hand and then takes

Holofernes's sword from its place near his bed. She grabs his hair and, striking twice, cleanly severs Holofernes's head. Leaving the body within the concealing canopy of the general's bed, Judith gives the grisly trophy to her maid who places it in their food bag.

Judith and the maid leave the camp, pretending that they are simply going to pray as Judith had done the three previous days, and then they return to Bethulia. Their cries to the gatekeeper to open the city gates for them attract a crowd carrying torches for light. Judith, praising God's intervention, draws the severed head from her bag and holds it up for all to see, saying, "The Lord has struck him down by the hand of a woman." She proclaims that it was Holofernes's lust that proved his undoing while she remained undefiled and without shame.

At her instruction, the head is hung from the parapet of the city wall, and the entire garrison of the city arms itself and musters for battle in front of the city. Achior is brought to identify the head as that of Holofernes. When he sees it hanging on the wall, he is overcome with emotion. Judith tells him how she killed the Assyrian general, and at that moment Achior is converted to a firm belief in the Israelite God and is circumcised.

At dawn, when the Assyrian sentries see that the Israelites are prepared for battle, Bagoas goes to inform Holofernes. Finding his master dead, he cries out in dismay that "one Hebrew woman has brought disgrace upon the house of King Nebuchadnezzar!" Without a leader, the Assyrians are thrown into complete disarray, and they flee in terror. The Israelites throughout the area are alerted, and they turn on their demoralized foe, chasing them as far as Damascus and slaughtering the great host of men. The Assyrian camp at Bethulia provides a huge harvest of booty—an enriching reward for the Israelites who spend 30 days plundering it.

Judith is given the tent of Holofernes and his silver furnishing as her share of the loot. She packs it all on mules and leads the animals to Jerusalem. Along the way, the men and women adorn themselves with garlands and olive wreaths and dance in celebration of the great victory. Finally, like Deborah (Judges 5), Judith sings a song of thanksgiving to God, acknowledging his hand in destroying the Assyrians and mocking the boastful enemy.

When the company arrives, Judith dedicates all that she has received to God. A three-month celebration before the Temple follows. After her return to Bethulia, Judith refuses all offers of marriage, choosing to remain a widow the rest of her days. She dies at age 105, having saved her people and serving much the same role as the judge Deborah had done.

Judith functions as a trickster figure in this story in much the same vein as Jacob or Esther. She stands as a model of proper behavior, but ironically can still lie and murder in order to save God's people. These themes and characters would have been very popular with the Jews during the Hellenistic period. Despite Judith's acknowledged accomplishments, however, it is likely that for the Jews during the Hellenistic period the most significant event in this story is actually the conversion to Yahweh worship of Achior the Ammonite. Such a conversion by a non-Israelite to Judaism highlights the power of Yahweh more than any military victory.

The Maccabean Revolt

❖ ❖ ❖

HISTORICAL BACKGROUND

THROUGHOUT THE THREE CENTURIES before the turn of the era, Jews were engaged in a struggle to maintain their religious heritage while adapting to an increasingly Greek world. How far could a Jew accommodate the Gentile world and still be considered faithful to the Law of Moses? Did it even matter anymore to be faithful to the Law? These questions concerned many Jews and were answered quite differently within the Jewish community. Some Jews formed tight communities in which it would be relatively easy to go on following the dietary laws and Sabbath regulations that characterized their lives. Others threw off the yoke of Torah in favor of the power and wealth that apostasy could bring in a Greek world.

One string of events within this larger struggle became particularly important for the shape of Jewish identity and had a significant effect on Jewish consciousness for centuries to come. This series of incidents occurred in Palestine during the years 175 to 142 B.C. At first, Jewish priests and aristocrats sought to settle the struggle in favor of adapting to the Greek way of life, believing this to be the way to put Jerusalem back on the world map as a progressive, cosmopolitan city. Their efforts were welcomed by the Syrian king Antiochus IV, who supported this initiative with his military forces. In their attempt to erase the Law of Moses, however, the Jewish aristocracy and Antiochus only succeeded in stirring up a zeal for Torah that expressed itself in a full-scale revolution against Gentile rule. These thirty years changed the shape of Palestine in many ways, and served to remind Jews everywhere just how important their heritage was to them.

The principal sources for this story are 1 and 2 Maccabees, which are found in the Old Testament apocrypha. Each tells the story to serve a specific purpose. First Maccabees, written around 90 B.C., supports the rule of the Hasmonean family (which came under heavy criticism) by reminding the people of the heroic exploits of that family's founders, namely Judas and his brothers. The author of this work seeks to revive the nation's sense of gratitude. Second Maccabees, written anywhere between 160 and 63 B.C., is more theologically oriented. It reaffirms the conviction that strict observance of the Law of Moses brings God's help and protection while neglect of that Law will bring national disaster. The real heroes of this story are the martyrs whose loyalty to God and God's Law restores God's favor to the whole nation.

ISRAEL "BECOMES LIKE THE NATIONS"

Between 332 and 323 B.C., Alexander the Great, son of Philip II of Macedon, unites all the people from Greece to Egypt to India under one ruler. As Alexander and his armies move from Greece southward and eastward, they plant communities patterned after Greek cities like Athens in each new conquered land. These cities contain Greek institutions like the *lyceum* and *gymnasium*, where the youth of the upper class are sent to be educated in the Greek language (the new language of politics and business), rhetoric, and athletics. They

143

also contain temples dedicated to Greek gods and goddesses, theaters for enjoying Greek literature and drama, and other buildings and spaces where the native population can be exposed to Greek philosophy and learning. The aristocracy of every conquered land eagerly enrolls their children in the Greek schools and seeks to adapt to the Greek way of life so that they might continue to enjoy high positions in the new regime.

Alexander dies in 323 B.C. at the age of 33, leaving no viable heir. His empire is split into four parts by his strongest generals, who found dynasties of their own. Two of these generals—Ptolemy I and Seleucus I—are important for the present story. Ptolemy and his successors rule Egypt and Palestine; Seleucus and his descendants govern Syria and Asia Minor. The Ptolemies, who control Judea from 319 to 198 B.C., allow Jews considerable peace and freedom to govern themselves according to their own law, the Torah. Some Jews, like Joseph from the house of Tobias, rise to considerable power and wealth by bending their observance of Torah in order to interact more freely with Gentile friends and patrons.

Antiochus III, the great-great-grandson of Seleucus I, makes several attempts to gain Palestine for his own empire, finally winning it in 198 B.C. at the battle of Panias. Judea is now under a new family of masters, but Antiochus III continues the tolerant policy that Judea had enjoyed under Persian, Greek, and Ptolemaic rule. The historian Josephus preserves a document written by Antiochus III in which the king gives Jews the legal right to continue self-governance by the Law of Moses. But matters will change dramatically under his son,

Antiochus IV, who enters into a partnership with certain Jewish priestly nobles to bring Jerusalem fully into the Greek world.

When Antiochus IV rises to the throne of Syria, Jerusalem is being supervised by Onias III, a high priest who is highly committed to maintaining loyalty to the Law of Moses. Other members of Onias's family, along with members of powerful rival families in Jerusalem, believe that his conservative tendencies are holding back Jerusalem's growth and prosperity. These families want to participate in the larger cultural life of the Mediterranean and enjoy free access to economic and political advancement in the larger arena of the Greek kingdoms. Onias is accused of mismanagement by a member of another noble family, and he must travel to Antioch to answer these charges before Antiochus himself. Onias has a brother named Jeshua, who wants to make Jerusalem more of a Greek city. While Onias is gone, therefore, Jeshua sends a large bribe to Antiochus petitioning for himself to be made high priest in place of his brother Onias. Antiochus IV, embracing Alexander's vision for one culture uniting his empire into one people, had encouraged the elites among his subjects to take on the Greek way of life. He also inherited from his father an enormous burden of debt in the form of an annual tribute owed to the Roman Republic (which, already being a formidable power, made the Syrian kings pay for the privilege of not being conquered). Both of these factors make Jeshua's offer very appealing.

Antiochus therefore deposes Onias and appoints Jeshua to the high priesthood. This is demoralizing for many Jews. The high priesthood was a sacred, hereditary office, and now it was being bought with bribes and appointed by Gentile overlords. Jeshua's policy, however, makes matters far worse. He changes his own name from Jeshua, after the Old Testament hero, to Jason, the hero of a Greek myth. Jason begins to transform Jerusalem into a Greek city, which he calls Antioch-at-Jerusalem. The Torah, the Law of Moses, is set aside as the law of the land. Henceforth, Jason proposes, Jerusalem will follow a Greek constitution patterned after the constitution of Athens. He builds a Greek school and gymnasium and enrolls young men from the wealthy families that support his policies. He also reorganizes the government according to the Greek pattern, which is democratic in that all citizens are permitted a voice in government—and very undemocratic in that only a small percentage of the population are actually citizens. Jason enrolls as citizens of Antioch-at-Jerusalem all those noble families that are supportive of his cause—and there are many families, even among the priesthood, that support his policy. Loyal, conservative Jews find themselves without a voice or a vote.

Jason enjoys three years in the office of high priest (175–172 B.C.). In 172, he sends a man named Menelaus, a member of a lower-ranking priestly family, to take the annual tribute to Antiochus and to attend to other business matters. Standing before Antiochus, Menelaus asks to be made high priest in place of Jason. Because he is supported by a powerful aristocratic family that rivals Jason's family, Menelaus is able to offer the king a vastly larger bribe than Jason. Antiochus, always looking for more income to finance his campaigns against Egypt and other activities, accepts the offer.

Once more, Jews are subject to the disgrace of seeing the high priesthood sold to the highest bidder. This time, however, matters are even worse. At least Jason had been in the line of Zadok, high priest in the time of Solomon and the founder of the chief priestly family. Menelaus, from the obscure priestly family of Bilga, had no such claim to the high priesthood. The episode must have been demoralizing indeed for the common people of Judea. Many members of the upper class and Jewish militia remain loyal to Jason, even though he is forced to flee from Jerusalem.

Jerusalem becomes a tense city. The event that finally causes it to erupt comes in 169 B.C., shortly after Antiochus begins a campaign against Egypt. A false rumor spreads that Antiochus has died in battle. Hearing this, Jason believes that his long-awaited opportunity to regain control of the high priesthood has arrived. He attacks Menelaus, forcing him and his supporters back into the citadel, a fortress built within Jerusalem. Jason, however, has aroused too much popular resentment on account of his attitude toward the treasured Torah and the Jewish way of life. He cannot sustain his attack and finds himself expelled once more from Jerusalem, eventually dying in exile. Menelaus seeks help from Antiochus who, hearing of the events in Jerusalem, believes that factions in Judea that favor Egyptian rule are revolting against him. He responds by marching his army to Jerusalem and slaughtering thousands of Jews.

Antiochus restores Menelaus, but Menelaus and his supporters are unable to gain the favor of the majority of Jerusalem's residents. In early 167, Syrian troops again enter Jerusalem, this time to stay. The soldiers occupy the citadel next to the Temple. Many residents of Jerusalem flee to the countryside; many more have their houses and property confiscated in order to furnish housing for the soldiers. The Temple itself becomes the common property of the Jewish and Gentile inhabitants of Antioch-at-Jerusalem. In keeping with the new philosophy of Hellenism, the Temple must also become more inclusive so as to serve the needs of Gentile as well as Jewish residents. The rituals of the Temple, therefore, are reworked to include elements from native Syrian cults. Many foreign gods are worshipped using foreign and forbidden rituals, turning the altar of the Temple in Jerusalem into the "abomination of desolation" (1 Maccabees 1:54; also see Daniel 11:31). The majority of Jews (except for Menelaus and his faction) desert the Temple, which has been polluted by these alien cults.

Most distressing of all, measures are now taken against those who wish to remain loyal to the Torah and ancestral religion of Israel. It had become clear to Menelaus and Antiochus that observance of the Jewish religion and civil unrest went hand-in-hand. They therefore initiate in Jerusalem a frightful persecution and an uncompromising program of forced apostasy. Circumcision, possession of copies of the Torah, and Sabbath observance are now prohibited under threat of death. The First Book of Maccabees describes mothers being executed with the infants they had circumcised, and old men being slaughtered while the scrolls of the Law of Moses they had hidden were burned. Stories in 2 Maccabees tell of an aged priest, seven brothers, and a

148

mother being tortured to death rather than eat a mouthful of pork as a symbolic rejection of their allegiance to the Jewish faith and way of life. This book credits the martyrs with playing a large part in bringing about a reversal in Israel's fortunes. Their faithfulness unto death turned aside God's anger and restored God's desire to protect his people. Officers of Antiochus and agents of Menelaus are sent out to enforce the prohibitions against Torah throughout Judea.

THE REVOLUTION OF JUDAS MACCABAEUS AND HIS BROTHERS

The scene is now set for the zealous acts of Mattathias, a member of a minor priestly family, and his five sons. The family comes to be referred to as the Hasmonean dynasty, from the name of Mattathias's great-grandfather, Hashmon. Mattathias and his family leave Jerusalem after the Torah is set aside as the law of the land. They settle in the village of Modein to avoid the defilement that has overtaken the capital city. Eventually, the officers of Antiochus and the agents of Menelaus are sent out from Jerusalem to enforce the prohibitions against keeping the Torah throughout Judea. When they arrive at Modein and assemble the residents of the village, the king's officer invites Mattathias, an elder and respected figure in the community, to be the first to offer sacrifice to a pagan deity as a sign of accepting the new policy. He promises Mattathias and his sons positions of honor and great wealth if they lead the way for their fellow villagers to join Menelaus's program. Mattathias staunchly refuses. When another Jew seizes the opportunity to gain favor in the eyes of the officer by coming forward to offer the sacrifice,

Mattathias kills him together with the king's officer. He then calls out: "Let everyone who is zealous for the Torah and supports the covenant come with me" (1 Maccabees 2:27). Mattathias gathers a force of freedom fighters who hide in the hills and strike out first at Jews in the villages who have renounced their loyalty to the Mosaic covenant.

After successfully defeating the oppressors, Judas Maccabaeus prays for the dead.

Mattathias dies in 166 B.C., leaving the command of the rebel forces to his middle son, Judas, who is so successful in battle that he earns the nickname "Maccabaeus"—the "hammer." Judas and his band of guerillas begin to take on the Syrian king's forces. Time after time, they beat larger and better-trained armies. With each victory, Judas's army draws out more supporters from those who wish to see their ancestral way of life preserved. Eventually, in 164 B.C. (after three years of fighting), Judas and his army liberate most of the city of

THE MIRACULOUS OIL

While the author of 2 Maccabees calls the festival by
the names "Purification of the Temple" or "Dedication
of the Altar," Hanukkah came to be known rather as the
"Feast of Lights," probably from the rise in importance of
the celebration in each Jewish family's home of lighting of
lamps, particularly an eight-branched candlestick. Each
branch of the candelabra marked a day of the festival. One
rabbinic school—the house of Shammai—observed this
tradition by lighting eight candles on the first day of the
feast, and extinguishing one
each day of the festival.
The house of Hillel,
another important
rabbinic school, lit one
light on the first night
of the festival, and one
additional light each
successive night.

This domestic ritual
gave rise to legends that
sought to explain the
practice, and also to
explain the shift in
emphasis from "Dedi-
cation" to "Lights."

*The eight-branched candlestick
known as a menorah is traditionally
used when celebrating Hanukkah.*

The most common of
these legends dates back to the Tanna'im of the second
century A.D. and is recorded in the tractate *Shabbat* 21b
of the Babylonian Talmud. When the time came for the
rededication of the Temple, the priests could only find a
single vial of oil that had not been defiled during the time
of apostasy. This vial ought to have kept the Temple cande-
labrum burning for only a single day, but it miraculously
kept the light burning for the full eight days of the festival.

Jerusalem from the control of the Gentile generals and the apostate priest Menelaus. The foreign invaders are only able to keep control of the citadel, the fortress beside the Temple, and Menelaus has to flee the city.

Judas selects a number of priests who remained faithful to the Torah. They build a new altar to replace the one that was defiled with pagan sacrifices. They ritually cleanse the Temple and fashion new bowls and vessels for the sacrifices. On the twenty-fifth day of Chislev (a winter month roughly corresponding to the second half of November and first half of December)—the very same day on which the Temple had been desecrated three years earlier—the priests offer holy sacrifices once more to the God of Israel. Judas and his supporters celebrate this rededication of the Temple and restoration of the Jewish religion in Jerusalem for eight days, and Jews have commemorated this triumph ever since in the festival of Hanukkah.

Through military and diplomatic endeavors over two decades, a rather undistinguished priestly family had risen to the hereditary claim of the offices of high priest and king in Judea. Once the dynasty is firmly in place with the accession of John Hyrcanus I, the son of Simon (Judas's last surviving brother), it continues in an unbroken line until 63 B.C. In that year, Antipater, father of Herod the Great, comes into effective control of Judea with the support of Pompey the Great and the Roman governor of Syria. Even though the history of the Hasmonean dynasty is marred by internal struggles and intrigue very much like the Syrian royal family, Judas and his brothers, at least, could truly be remembered as saviors of Judaism in Palestine.

Tales From Egyptian Judaism

❖   ❖   ❖   ❖

HISTORICAL BACKGROUND

IT IS ESTIMATED that six out of seven Jews lived outside of Palestine in what is called the "Diaspora," or "scattering," of the twelve tribes. The largest community of Jews in the Diaspora could be found in Alexandria, Egypt, a major center of learning and culture in the ancient world. Jews living in the Diaspora and, it seems, particularly in Alexandria, faced tension on two fronts. On the one hand, many Gentiles harbored prejudice against Jews on account of peculiarities in the Jewish religion. In a world of many gods, strict devotion to One God to the exclusion of all others seemed to be kin to atheism. On the other hand, Diaspora Jews appear to have been sensitive about comments made by their own fellow Jews in Palestine. Many Jews, whose families had lived outside Palestine for generations, had forgotten the Hebrew language and so relied on a Greek translation of their sacred Scriptures. Palestinian Jews saw this as an imperfect translation of the Word of God, and questioned whether or not the Law could be perfectly followed where it was not available in its original language. Furthermore, since the original scattering of Jews from Israel to the lands of the Gentiles (721–587 B.C.) was viewed as divine punishment, the very fact of continued living outside the Holy Land was seen as a sign of God's lingering displeasure. This even led Jews

The Scriptures were translated from Hebrew into several Greek versions (also known as the "Septuagint").

in Palestine to tell Jews in the Diaspora that they were praying for them, so that God would eventually be reconciled to them (see 2 Maccabees 1:1–9).

Jews in the Diaspora, however, did not see themselves as living outside of Palestine because God was still displeased with them. They had known centuries of God's favor and friendship in their new countries, and believed themselves to be as close to God's heart living in Egypt or in Rome as were their fellow Jews living in

Jerusalem. Moreover, they felt that their Greek translation of the Scriptures allowed them to know God's revelation and his will as clearly and perfectly as the Hebrew original. It is not surprising to find, therefore, that Jews in Alexandria wrote stories to affirm their own place in God's favor and to promote the reliability and authority of their version of the Scriptures. Alongside these concerns, the same literature affirms that the Jewish way of life is every bit as enlightened as, and indeed superior to, the way of life followed by Greeks or any other Gentile group. *Third Maccabees* and the *Letter of Aristeas to Philocrates* admirably accomplish both goals.

PTOLEMY AND THE JEWS

The story of 3 Maccabees opens in the year 217 B.C. with Ptolemy IV, king of Egypt, advancing against the forces of Antiochus III, king of Syria. The armies meet at Raphia on the coast of the Mediterranean, just south of Palestine. Ptolemy defeats Antiochus III, who retreats with his armies back to Syria. The Egyptian monarch then tours the cities in that region in order to reassure them in the wake of the war and to assure himself that the people will remain loyal to him. As was customary for a ruler in the ancient world, Ptolemy seeks to bolster morale by visiting the temples held sacred by his subjects and making generous donations to the temple treasuries. This policy meets with tremendous success until Ptolemy arrives at Jerusalem and tries to do the same there. Local law (the Torah, the Law of Moses) forbids any Gentile to set foot in the inner courts of the Temple. Ptolemy, however, proposes to go into the Most Holy Place, where only the Jewish high priest is allowed to go once each year on the Day of Atonement

Ptolemy II fought against the Seleucids and had the Bible translated to Greek.

(Yom Kippur). The residents of Jerusalem gather in the streets to protest this impending pollution of the Temple and to pray for God's help. When at last Simon, the High Priest, adds his voice to theirs, Ptolemy is physically attacked by God and left temporarily comatose. His bodyguards remove him from the Temple. After recovering, Ptolemy returns to Egypt, preparing to take revenge upon the Jewish population in his own land for what happened to him in Jerusalem.

Ptolemy believes that the source of his troubles is what he perceives to be the strange and intolerant customs of the Jews. He therefore plans to make his homeland safe by extending the privilege of full Alexandrian citizenship (a great honor with many practical advantages) to any Jew who would begin to participate in some Greek form of religion. This would demonstrate their solidarity with Ptolemy and his government. Those Jews who refuse, however, will be reduced to the status of slaves. A surprisingly small number of Jews accept the king's offer (about three hundred), while the rest prefer to suffer loss of status and freedom rather than abandon their covenant with God. Indeed, the faithful Jews openly show their contempt for the apostates who accept the king's offer. Hearing of this, Ptolemy decides that the race is too vicious to keep around even as slaves, so he assembles all the Jews living in his kingdom (except for those who had con-

THIRD MACCABEES

A work of "historical fiction," 3 Maccabees was written in Greek by a Jew residing in Egypt, most likely Alexandria. Based on similarities with phrases from official edicts dating from 160–60 B.C., as well as signs of dependence on Esther and 2 Maccabees, the book is dated to the first half of the first century B.C. The book is associated with the other books of the Maccabees mainly on account of similarity of the plot; none of the Maccabean family, or any other characters from 1 and 2 Maccabees for that matter, appears in this story.

Third Maccabees is especially valuable as a witness to sources of anti-Jewish sentiments in the ancient world, as well as Jewish responses to that hostility. The Law of Moses called for worship of the God of Israel alone, as well as for obedience to certain dietary restrictions and purity codes. Because of these restrictions, devout Jews tended to stand apart from the rest of their neighbors, and these Gentile neighbors interpreted their separateness as arrogance, hatred of foreigners, and even as signs of potential sedition. The larger community felt as though the Jews in their midst were not fellow citizens concerned about the common good of the city nor reliable friends. Conversely, the Jewish author of 3 Maccabees criticizes Gentiles as people whose minds are "alienated from the truth" concerning God and whose actions toward God's loyal people are "arrogant." Differences in values and customs thus led to deep suspicion and prejudice on both sides. Finally, the story shows the intense mutual hatred that existed between Jews who adhered to the Law of Moses and Jews who pursued the advantages of accommodating to Greek values and lifestyle.

verted to the Greek way of life) for execution in the stadium at Alexandria.

The story now tells of God's protection of his faithful people. Even before they offer a prayer, God is at work helping them. While the lists of Jewish names are being drawn up, the king's scribes run out of paper and ink so they cannot complete their task. This allows some people, whose names are not on the list, to avoid danger. A great number of Jews, however, are still herded into the stadium to await their death. Ptolemy plans a feast for his courtiers while they await the entertainment: the spectacle of military elephants, drugged with wine and incense, trampling the Jews. But in response to the prayers of the victims, God causes Ptolemy to remain asleep through the entire day. The crowd is dismissed, and the Jews have another day of life. When the preparations are repeated, God causes Ptolemy to become so disoriented that he forgets his plan and inquires angrily why such loyal subjects as the Jews should be treated in this manner. Confused, his guests retire once more. On the third day, the king repeats the preparations, and this time does release the armored elephants on the Jews. The sight fills the victims with fear, but an old priest, named Eleazar, silences their screams and prays to God for deliverance. In response, God's angels appear and so frighten the elephants that they turn around and trample Ptolemy's soldiers.

Ptolemy repents of his plan and blames his courtiers for urging him on in this unjust and unprofitable act. He sets the Jews free and provides magnificently for their return with a seven-day feast. Ptolemy issues a decree that protects Jewish rights and customs and allows those Jews who had remained faithful to their religion to cleanse their community by killing the apostates.

Mary and Joseph

❖ ❖ ❖

BIBLICAL BACKGROUND

THE GOSPEL ACCOUNTS of Jesus' annunciation and birth (found in the books of Matthew and Luke) center on his importance as the Son of God. Mary is a vehicle for the Incarnation, but other than her song, the *Magnificat* (Luke 1:46–55), she has little to say in the narrative. Joseph is even more of a shadowy character, providing a home and legal protection to Mary and the child Jesus, but little else. Naturally, this gave rise to speculation about Mary and Joseph, their lives prior to the birth of Jesus, and incidents that occurred shortly after Jesus' birth. Such an important couple deserved more attention than was to be found in the official accounts, so extrabiblical accounts were written to fill in the gaps.

THE *PROTEVANGELIUM OF JAMES*

A number of apocryphal works were produced that attempted to fill in some of the details about Mary and Joseph. One of the most popular was the *Protevangelium of James* (abbrev. *PJ*) that dates to the mid to late second century A.D. The author claims to be James, the brother of Jesus, but a lack of knowledge about Jewish customs and a clear misunderstanding of Palestinian geography indicate that the author may have been a Syrian or Egyptian Christian. Most surviving manuscripts are written in Greek, although its popularity is indicated by the many translations that exist and its citation in the works of such important early Church Fathers as Origen (d. 254) and Clement of Alexandria (early third century). This work continued to be used as part of popular theology in the Eastern Orthodox Church for many centuries. However, it was condemned by Jerome for its mention of Joseph's previous marriage and children prior to his marriage to Mary. As a result, the Western Church, based in Rome, attempted to suppress it, but *PJ* still had an impact on the growth of the theological importance of the Virgin Mary.

The Life of Mary

The story found in *PJ* is an attempt to provide the figure of Mary with a miraculous (although not immaculate) birth narrative. In this way, she receives her proper due as the mother of Jesus. The tale begins with a familiar theme, an old barren couple who miraculously receive a child from God. Joachim and Anna are righteous and God-fearing, but they have no children.

Answered Prayers

Each of the elements in the story of Joachim and Anna is reminiscent of stories in the Old Testament and in other ancient Near Eastern literature. In the Ugaritic epic of Aqhat (1600 B.C.), the righteous king Danil prays fervently to the gods and makes special sacrifices to them for seven days before they respond affirmatively to his plea for a son. In the story of Samson's parents, they learn of the birth of their son from an angel who appears to them separately (Judges 13:2–23), just as in the case of Anna and Joachim. Similarly, both Anna and Hannah, the mother of Samuel, promise to dedicate their hoped-for child to God's service if the Lord will open their wombs and allow them to conceive (1 Samuel 1:9–11).

Mary, the mother of Jesus, was born miraculously to Joachim and Anna, who had been barren.

To cleanse any possible sin from his spirit and to entreat God without any distractions, Joachim spends 40 days and 40 nights in the wilderness (compare Jesus in Matthew 4:2). For her part, Anna dresses in mourning garments and laments the fact that she is unfulfilled. Their prayers are answered by an angel who predicts the birth of a child and promises that this infant "shall be spoken of in the whole world."

When Anna gives birth, she proclaims "my soul is magnified this day," (compare Luke 1:46) and names the child Mary. The special nature of this child then is demonstrated by her being able to walk at six months. As a way of setting Mary apart from other children and protecting her purity, Joachim creates a kind of "sanctuary" within his house for her. He also employs the willing service of Hebrew virgins who come to care for her. Their virginity is a model of Mary's nature and signifies her eventual role as Christ's mother. At her presentation in the temple on her first birthday, the chief priests, scribes, and elders bless her, while Anna, the aged mother, rejoices in her ability to nurse Mary and sings a song of thanksgiving (compare Elizabeth's prayer in Luke 1:25).

As Mary grows older, her parents must make the decision to present her to God as Anna had promised. They delay this task until the child is three years old and no longer is dependent on her mother (compare Samuel's presentation when he is weaned; 1 Samuel 1:22–28). Mary is taken to the temple in procession with torch-bearing virgins and is greeted by the high priest with a kiss and a blessing, predicting that "because of you the Lord at the end of the days will reveal his redemption to the sons of Israel."

Mary remains as a ward in the temple, being fed by the hand of an angel, until her 12th year. At that point, as she nears puberty, the priests take council because once her menstrual

Mary's parents bring her to the temple for her presentation to God.

cycle begins she can no longer remain within the temple precincts (Leviticus 15:19–30). In order to determine God's will, Zacharias, the high priest, goes into the Holy of Holies (the inner precinct in the temple) where an angel tells him to assemble all the widowers of the land. God will then indicate which of this company is chosen to become Mary's husband.

The priests gather each man's rod, and the high priest prays over them within the temple. The rods are then returned one by one. When Joseph the carpenter receives his rod, a dove emerges from it and comes to rest on his head, indicating that he is the chosen one of God. When presented with Mary as his ward by the high priest, Joseph is embarrassed and asks to be forgiven this responsibility. He says that he is an old man with sons by his first wife, and he does not wish to "become a laughingstock" among his neighbors. Zacharias warns him against attempting to cast aside God's command, and Joseph relents. However, as soon as he has taken Mary home, Joseph leaves her to continue work on several building projects, saying "the Lord will guard you." The *Gospel of Pseudo-Matthew* adds here that Mary is accompanied to Joseph's house by six virgins so that she does not go unchaperoned and will not be left completely alone while Joseph is away.

The next step by the author of the *Protevangelium of James* to create an image of perfection for Mary comes when the priests decide to commission the weaving of a veil for the temple. Only virgins of the lineage of David are allowed to participate, and at this point the reader is told that Mary is of that lineage. This may have been an answer to early criticism in the church that Matthew's genealogy for Joseph (Matthew 1:1–16) was insufficient proof of Jesus' kinship tie to David. If Mary is also given a Davidic lineage, however, these concerns are addressed and defused.

Given one of the favored tasks in the weaving process, Mary is interrupted in her work by an angel who tells her that she will miraculously conceive and bear the "Son of the Most High." Her initial willingness to serve as the "handmaid of the Lord" is similar to the canonical story (see Luke 1:31). However, the story then brings out a more human set of reactions—shock and fear. Mary goes to visit her cousin Elizabeth, who is pregnant with John the Baptist. Elizabeth addresses her as "the mother of my Lord," but somehow Mary has forgotten what the angel had told her. Mary is perplexed and afraid when she realizes that she is supposed to remain a virgin until marriage and yet is pregnant at age 16.

Mary hides herself from view, but Joseph returns as she enters her sixth month and there is no way to prevent him from seeing her condition. Joseph berates himself for leaving her alone and thus open to temptation and defilement. When

Mary goes to visit her cousin Elizabeth, who is pregnant with John the Baptist.

Mary assures him, tearfully, that she has not "known" a man, he is even more confused. After thinking it over, he plans to quietly "put her away," but this idea is immediately set aside when an angel appears and tells him the child is "of the Holy Spirit."

Despite Joseph's belief in Mary, the priests are not convinced. They accuse Mary of failing to uphold her honor, and they accuse Joseph of taking advantage of his ward, consummating their marriage without the benefit of a ceremony before the people. When Mary and Joseph continue to plead their innocence, the priests administer the "water of conviction" to each of them, leaving it up to God to determine their guilt (see Numbers 5:12–22 for this method of trial by ordeal). Both pass the test without any sign of sin being displayed on their bodies, and the people rejoice at the power of God made manifest.

The census of Caesar Augustus (Luke 2:1) forces Joseph and Mary to travel to Bethlehem, but before they reach the town Mary goes into labor. Joseph finds a cave where she may give birth and goes to seek a midwife. During his search, Joseph experiences a miraculous stoppage of motion around him. Sheep are frozen in place, a shepherd stands with his staff raised, and birds are stopped in mid-flight. Then, just as suddenly, all returns to normal and the midwife appears. Joseph tells her about Mary and brings her to the cave. However, before she can assist the birth, a cloud hides the cave and then a bright light appears blinding them temporarily. When it dims, the child has been born and the midwife cries out in astonishment.

PJ then repeats the story of the three wise men and their following a star so bright that it outshines all others. Herod's anger and concern lead to the slaughter of all babies under two years old. While no mention is made here of Mary and Joseph's flight to Egypt, the narrative does describe how Elizabeth is able to save the infant John the Baptist from Herod's men. She climbs into the hills, and when she can go no farther she prays and the "mountain is rent asunder," and a light held by an angel guides them to safety.

When he cannot find John, Herod has his officers question Zacharias, John's father. He denies any knowledge of where his son has gone, and Herod orders Zacharias's execution. He is killed before the altar in the temple (see reference to this story in Matthew 23:35). However, only his blood, now turned to stone, can be found since his body had disappeared. A voice tells the frightened priests of Zacharias's murder, and three days of mourning follow. The narrative then concludes with the appointment of Symeon as the new high priest. A note is added that he has received a message from the Holy Spirit that he would not die until he has seen Christ "in the flesh" (see Luke 2:25–26). In

THE *HISTORY OF JOSEPH THE CARPENTER*

The *History of Joseph the Carpenter (Hst-J)* is another apocryphal narrative that deals with the parents of Jesus and is dependent on the *Protevangelium of James*. It was first written in Greek, but survives as a Coptic text and thus is probably an Egyptian work. While its exact date of composition is unknown, some scholars suggest the fourth or fifth century. A later date, however, is suggested by its emphasis on the feast day of Joseph, something that was not established in the canonical calendar until a few centuries later.

this way, the continuity of priestly leadership is tied to Christ's coming mission.

THE *GOSPEL OF PSEUDO-MATTHEW*

The amount of additional information on the early life of Mary continued to grow during the centuries of the Medieval church. Among the works produced was the *Gospel of Pseudo-Matthew* (abbrev. *Ps-M*), which elaborates on previous sets of stories, such as *PJ*, augmenting the narrative in places.

Among the unique additions of *Ps-M* is an encounter Joseph and Mary have on their way to Bethlehem. Mary says she has had a vision of two persons, one weeping and one rejoicing. Joseph thinks she is merely jabbering and discounts what she says. But then a young man (an angel) appears. He scolds Joseph and tells them that the vision is of the "Jews weeping because they have departed from their God" and of the "Gentiles rejoicing because they are now...near to the Lord."

Ps-M describes the flight to Egypt to escape Herod in some detail. This story is filled with miraculous events, including several occasions when Jesus saves his parents from menacing beasts. In one episode, they are accosted by dragons, but the infant Jesus climbs down from his mother's lap and stands before the beasts. They fall down and worship him and then retire to their cave (see Psalm 148:7). When his parents exclaim that Jesus must not place himself in such danger, he replies he is not a mere child "for I have always been and even now am perfect." Later attacks by lions, leopards, and wolves end the same way with the beasts worshiping Jesus.

Another miraculous event occurs when the group is forced to rest because Mary is overcome by the heat. Mary notices a palm tree laden with fruit, and she expresses a desire to eat some of it. Jesus causes the palm tree to bow down so that Mary can reach its fruit. He also has one of its roots tap a water source so that Joseph's concern over their empty water bags will be met. The tree is rewarded by having a branch taken by an angel to be transplanted in Paradise. Stories such as these serve the purpose of demonstrating Jesus' respect for his parents while maintaining proof of his lordship over creation.

When they reach Egypt, Mary and the child enter a temple. As they set foot in the door, the 365 idols housed there are cast from their pedestals and broken (compare 1 Samuel 5:1–5). The local governor and all the people are so overcome by this sign of God's supremacy that they fall down and worship, acknowledging their belief "in the Lord God through Jesus Christ." Mary's role as the bearer of Christ is also highlighted since she is always described as holding Jesus to her breast as the people worship him.

THE DEATH OF JOSEPH

An abbreviated version of the narrative in *PJ* is found in the *History of Joseph the Carpenter (Hst-J)*. The primary concern of this work, narrated by Jesus, is to describe the death of Joseph at the advanced age of 111 and again to have one of Jesus' parents acknowledge his true nature.

Jesus and Mary sit with Joseph on his deathbed, one at his head and the other at his feet. Mary finds that Joseph's feet are as cold as ice, and she realizes that he is near death. She then calls her daughter Lydia to join her in the mourning lament. When Death approaches to take Joseph away, Jesus rebukes him and holds him at bay, behind the door, while they all pray that the journey Joseph's soul must travel will be a safe one, that the "river of fire be as water and the sea of demons cease vexing." In his last moments, the old man makes his confession of faith in Jesus as the Son of God. He also asks forgiveness for doubting Mary's purity since he was ignorant of the circumstances of Jesus' conception. When Joseph dies, the angels Michael and Gabriel shroud Joseph's body in a shining cloth and preserve his soul from the demons of darkness until he could be conducted into the "dwelling place of the pious."

After Jesus tells them the story of Joseph's death, some of the apostles ask him why Joseph could not have been spared death like Enoch and Elijah. Jesus tells them that even these two witnesses of events on earth will eventually have to die, victims of the venom of the Antichrist. This mention of the "two witnesses" parallels the account in Revelation 11:1–7 and ties this work into the apocalyptic expectations of many Christians.

Stories of Jesus' Infancy

❖ ❖ ❖

BIBLICAL BACKGROUND

Luke's statement that "the child grew and became strong" (Luke 2:40) simply did not satisfy the need of early Christians to know more about their Savior's childhood. Certainly, the story of his presentation in the Temple and his conversation at age twelve with the elders (Luke 2:41–52) was interesting and helped fill in a small gap in the period between Jesus' birth and the beginning of his ministry, but it also served to whet the appetite of believers for more. When reliable information from the official accounts failed to give them what they felt they needed, the storytellers wove legends that eventually supplied most of the missing details. The

INFANCY NARRATIVES

There are a number of Infancy Narratives that date to the second through sixth centuries A.D. For instance, the *Arabic Infancy Gospel* is of Egyptian origin, was probably written originally in Syriac in the fifth century, and survives in a number of manuscripts as well as in the 13th-century "History of the Virgin." It is dependent for some of its material on the *Protevangelium of James (PJ)* and the *Infancy Story of Thomas*. The *Life of John the Baptist* also contains some infancy material. The author claims that the document was written in Greek by the Egyptian bishop Serapion at the end of the fourth century, but it survives in Syriac manuscripts.

After an angel appears to Joseph, he and his family, including the infant Jesus, flee to Egypt to escape Herod's deadly wrath.

growing popularity of these legendary stories during the Middle Ages can be seen in two ways: (1) the occasional suppression of this material by the leaders of the Church, and (2) an explosion of religious art depicting such stories as Jesus' birth in a cave and Mary spinning a portion of the Temple veil.

JESUS IN EGYPT

The flight to Egypt was undertaken to save Jesus from Herod's plan to kill all the infants in Bethlehem (Matthew 2:16–18). Although no mention is made in the Gospels of what transpired in Egypt, the apocryphal Infancy Stories contain numerous tales of the miracles the child Jesus performed. Most of these episodes are designed to show Jesus' mercy to the poor and afflicted.

Among the tales in the *Arabic Infancy Gospel* is one about Jesus' bathwater. After the child has been cleansed, a woman stores the water and later pours it on a girl who has leprosy. The girl is immediately cured, and the townspeople exclaim that Jesus and his parents "are gods, not men." In a similar story, water from a spring is used to wash Jesus' shirt. As Mary wrings out the sweat from the laundered shirt, balsam appears in that place.

After leaving the village in which they had been staying, the holy couple are captured in the desert by a gang of robbers. One, named Titus, asks his fellow robber Dumachus to help him free Mary and Joseph and the child. Dumachus refuses until Titus pays him 40 drachma. After their escape, Jesus tells his mother that in 30 years these two robbers will be crucified on either

THE *INFANCY STORY OF THOMAS*

The most complete text describing Jesus' early childhood is found in the *Infancy Story of Thomas* (not to be confused with the Coptic Gospel of Thomas, which simply contains sayings attributed to Jesus and is not a narrative). The earliest versions of this document were written in Syriac and Greek, but a number of Latin manuscripts also exist. What is interesting to note is that each manuscript slightly differs from the others, suggesting that there were multiple traditions and versions circulating and that copyists felt free to add material that they felt rightly expanded the stories. Its earliest date of composition is the second century A.D., but one may presume that stories were added for at least two more centuries. The author, using Thomas's name to add authority to the document, was probably a Gentile Christian.

side of him and that the kind Titus will be allowed to enter Paradise (see Luke 23:32–43).

JESUS THE MIRACLE-WORKING CHILD

The *Infancy Story of Thomas* describes additional episodes about Jesus from ages five through twelve. Like the *Protevangelium of James*, this document chronicles a series of miracles by Jesus. However, *PJ* is always careful to tie each miracle, such as the submission of dragons and other beasts, to Jesus' mastery of creation, therefore making it a justification for his worship. Similarly, *Pseudo-Matthew's* infancy material attempts to show Jesus as master over Egypt's gods when their images are cast down and broken as Jesus and Mary enter a temple. *Thomas*, on the other hand, portrays a child Jesus who learns how to control his powers as he matures. Certainly, some of the stories were told for their entertainment value and have less concern for ethical issues. In fact, some depict Jesus as an aloof and knowing child, who strikes out at ignorance and is very frightening to his parents, teachers, and playmates. However, the apparent theme here is to show Jesus experiencing some of the same phases of development that all children must pass through.

Perhaps because many Christians were experiencing persecution at the hands of powerful individuals and kings, the authors of the Infancy Stories may have speculated about how Jesus handled his extraordinary powers as a child. This may explain why there is an obvious maturing process that takes place in the stories. Thus the five-year-old Jesus uses divine powers almost indiscriminately and without thought, while the more meditative twelve-year-old Jesus considers his actions much

Many extrabiblical sources expand on Jesus' childhood, relating stories of his powers as well as his relationship with his parents.

more carefully. The opening tale has Jesus, like many little boys, playing beside a stream of water. He creates separate small pools of water, cleanses the water with a word, and then shapes seven sparrows from the clay and water of his pools. His almost absentminded creative acts recall God's creation of Adam in Genesis 2:4–7.

The problem is that Jesus has done this on the Sabbath and, as is so often the case in his later ministry, the Jews complain that he is violating the law (see Matthew 12:1–12; Mark 3:2–4). When Joseph comes to Jesus and asks him why he has done this "work" on the Sabbath, Jesus simply claps his hands, cries "Off with you!" and the clay sparrows come to life and fly away. The Jews are amazed by this sight and go to tell the elders.

While their attention is following the birds, the son of Annas the scribe takes a willow branch and destroys

Jesus' pools. This makes Jesus very angry. He calls the boy a "godless dunderhead" and then curses him, causing him to be withered up like an old man. The stricken boy's parents carry him away and reproach Joseph for having a child capable of doing things like this.

Another example of Jesus reacting angrily occurs when a boy runs past him and brushes Jesus' shoulder. In exasperation, Jesus stops the boy in his tracks with a word, and the child drops dead immediately. The grieving parents cannot believe that such a thing could happen just by speaking angry words, and they warn Joseph that he will be driven from the village if he does not teach his son to control such power to curse. When Joseph attempts to instruct Jesus, the child absolves his father, saying that Joseph is not speaking his own words, but those of others. Then the people who had pressured Joseph are struck with blindness. Joseph cannot take any more, and he grabs Jesus by the ear hoping to get Jesus' attention and prevent any further damage, but Jesus simply tells Joseph not to "vex" him.

Such behavior, lacking any apparent respect for his elders, brings Zacchaeus the teacher into the narrative. He tells Joseph that he will take the child and instruct him in his letters as well as in the proper way of addressing his elders. However, Jesus scorns Zacchaeus's ability to teach him anything. As they study the Greek alphabet, Jesus tells his teacher that he does not know even the first thing about the true nature of Alpha (the first Greek letter) so how can he dare to go on to Beta (the second Greek letter)? Jesus then presents an allegorical explanation of Alpha's shape and properties that completely confounds Zacchaeus. He takes Jesus back to Joseph, saying "I strove to get a disciple, and have found myself with a teacher!" Jesus responds favorably to this humbling speech by Zacchaeus. He graciously heals all those children and their parents who had been afflicted by his word.

On two other occasions, teachers attempt to instruct Jesus, with very different results. The first tries pedantically to force Jesus to repeat his alphabet over and over. Jesus sees no value in this rote memorization, and when he refuses to respond to his teacher's urging, the man strikes Jesus on the head. Jesus curses him and leaves him in a coma. Joseph, fearing the reaction of the neighbors, quickly takes Jesus home and hides him. The second teacher, however, is much more understanding of Jesus' abilities. When Jesus, with the help of the Holy Spirit, expounds authoritatively on the law to a large crowd, the teacher praises Jesus. He tells a frightened Joseph that the boy is full of grace and wisdom. And, because this man has spoken wisely, Jesus heals the foolish teacher.

The next episode again involves a testing of Jesus' powers and once again demands that the people acknowledge his word as supreme. While Jesus is playing with another child in the upper story of a house, his companion falls from a window and is killed. The parents, perhaps hoping to rid themselves of a troublemaker, accuse Jesus of pushing the child to his death. Jesus simply replies, "I did not throw him down." No one believes him, so Jesus leaps down beside the body of the dead boy, calls him by name, and instructs him to arise and tell everyone whether Jesus had pushed him. Miraculously, the boy gets up and affirms Jesus' innocence. Jesus is thus shown to display the same power to raise the dead that he will employ during his ministry (see Matthew 9:18–26; Luke 7:11–17).

There is a final set of miracle stories contained in *Thomas*, each one showing Jesus' growing maturity and concern for others. Some, like the story of Jesus carrying water in his cloak when he falls and breaks his mother's water jar, display a small child's solution to a problem. In another case, Jesus shows his father that his powers can have a practical benefit. Joseph had received a commission to fashion a bed for a rich man. However, when the sections for a bed are cut, one beam is longer than the other. Jesus then steps in to help his father by miraculously stretching the shorter piece of wood so that both now match.

Domestic miracles are amusing to the audience and suggest Jesus' future potential to help all people. But it is in the stories where Jesus relieves suffering that his true maturity is demonstrated. For example, when a woodcutter wounds himself with his ax and is bleeding to death, Jesus runs forward and heals the injured foot. Similarly, when a viper bites Joseph's son James, Jesus breathes on the venom mark and James is cured while the snake bursts. Another time, Jesus hears the cries of mourning when a small child dies. He immediately runs to the house and revives the child, saying, "Do not die but live and be with your mother." He also raises a young man who had been killed in a construction accident. Such acts of charity show a mature harnessing of his power and emotions. No longer is Jesus shown to wield power and act on instinct. In these final stories he sets a tone very similar to that in the Gospels.

Stories of Jesus' Ministry

◈ ◈ ◈ ◈

Biblical Background

AS IS SO OFTEN THE CASE with public figures, the official narrative about their lives is an abridged one. The writers of the Gospels shaped the stories in such a way that Jesus' message and his signs of power (miracles) were highlighted. There was surely much more that could be said about the three years of Jesus' public ministry, but decisions were made to include only what we now see as the Scriptures. What follows are the "other stories" about Jesus that somehow never got into the Gospels but still survived to add color and additional dimensions to the founder of Christianity. They, in large part, represent the Gospels used by several of the Jewish-Christian communities during the first three centuries of the Christian era. They are

Jesus is baptized by John the Baptist while the Holy Spirit descends upon him like a dove.

cited in the works of the early Church Fathers (Origen, Clement, Jerome, Eusebius, and Epiphanius), are in most cases variants on the canonical Gospel of Matthew, and include some heretical beliefs that would eventually be condemned by the Church Councils. Some of these variations on the Gospel story are the result of Christian communities borrowing elements of other religions and their sacred stories and blending them with the narratives about Jesus. In some cases, this was done to make conversion to Christianity easier, and in other cases it may be the result of an attempt to further enhance Jesus' position as the Son of God.

The Gospel of the Nazareans

Aside from a few fragments, all that is known of the *Gospel of the Nazareans* (*GN*) comes from citations in various Church Fathers' works and in their commentaries on books of the New Testament. For example, Jerome, the translator of the Latin Vulgate edition and premier scholar of the latter half of the fourth century A.D., cites a passage from *GN* indicating that Jesus, despite the urging of his mother, did not intend to be baptized by John the Baptist, saying "Wherein have I sinned that I should go and be baptized by him?" This stands in stark contrast to Matthew 3:13–15 in which Jesus has to convince John to baptize him.

Similarly, in his commentary on the story of the man with the withered hand (Matthew 12:9–13), Jerome cites the *GN* where it adds the information that the man was a mason. His plea to Jesus to heal him is based on his desire to return to his profession and earn a living rather than continue to exist as a beggar. An eighth- or ninth-century source notes that the *GN* names this mason

Malchus. While these are relatively minor additions, they do serve to flesh out the story of an anonymous sufferer. Giving the man a profession and a name makes it easier for the listener or the reader to identify with his pain and perhaps to associate it with their own.

Occasionally, these citations appear to be trying to answer a question that has either been asked by one of the Church Fathers' students or was a long-standing query. An example of this may be a note in a 14th-century text describing Jesus' passion narrative. In John 18:15–16, while Jesus is being questioned by Caiaphas, the high priest, Peter and "another disciple known to the high priest" stood outside. The *GN* supplies the information that the unnamed disciple is John and that he is known to the high priest because his father Zebedee had often sent him to the high priest's palace with fish for their table. It also notes here that Peter was not only standing outside the door, but he was weeping loudly before he was allowed to come into the palace.

An anti-Jewish bias is illustrated in some of these fragments. In one case the story of Jesus' scourging by the Roman soldiers (Mark 15:15) is expanded to include the accusation that Jews had bribed the four soldiers to beat Jesus even more severely than usual. Thus his blood flows "from every part of his body." These same four men are also bribed to inflect greater cruelty as they crucify Jesus (see John 19:17–24).

Some final variations noted in the *GN* include the statement that after Jesus absolves his executioners ("Father, forgive them, for they know not what they do"—Luke 23:34), thousands of those standing around the cross are converted to Christianity. One Church

Father, Haimo of Auxerre, says it is thousands of Jews who are converted, while a 14th-century Medieval source points to the 3,000 people converted on the day of Pentecost (Acts 2:41) and an additional 5,000 at a later date (Acts 4:4). In addition, the signs of mourning at the moment of Jesus' death, expressed by unnatural darkness and the tearing of the temple veil in Luke 23:44–45, is replaced in the *GN* by the splitting of the huge lintel stone of the temple and the wailing of disembodied voices. This latter variation on the traditional story is also found in Josephus. Since the lintel would have been in full view of the public (the veil was seen only by the priests within the temple), it would have been a much better piece of evidence of Jesus' importance and power.

THE GOSPEL OF THE EBIONITES

The *Gospel of the Ebionites* (*GE*) represents a variant gospel that reflects the views of the Jewish-Christian Ebionite community. They retain some aspects of their Jewish heritage—evidence of this can be seen in the story of Jesus' choosing his 12 disciples. This recounting resembles that in Luke 6:13–16, although it is written with Jesus as the narrator. As is the case in the canonical Gospels, the number 12 is emphasized, demonstrating a parallel with the 12 tribes of Israel and the Jewish origin of each document.

However, many of the Ebionite ideas would later be considered heretical. For instance, since the Ebionites denied the doctrine of the Virgin Birth, Jesus is portrayed as only a man until he is invested with divine power when the Holy Spirit unites with him at the time of his baptism by John the Baptist (based on Matthew 3:14–17). The "Christ" is therefore created by this union and Jesus at that point, rather than through the incarnation with Mary, becomes a divine being. In this episode, the voice from heaven proclaims Jesus to be "my Beloved Son" when Jesus emerges from the water and again when John questions Jesus to ascertain who he is. Further clarifying this position, the Ebionites are also said to deny that Christ was "begotten of God the Father," but was "created as one of the archangels" to rule over all the other angels and all the creatures of God. In this way, the nativity stories are completely set aside and Jesus' role as the bearer of a new revelation directly from God is reinforced.

John the Baptist is also portrayed in a slightly different way, with his traditional diet reduced from locust and wild honey (Matthew 3:4) to simply honey. This emphasizes the vegetarian doctrine of the Ebionite community. A further sign of this adherence to a vegetarian diet is found in Jesus' refusal to eat the meat of the Passover meal at the Last Supper (compare Luke 22:15). By having him refuse to eat meat, and by having Jesus say that he has "come to do away with sacrifices," they emphasize Jesus' role as the ultimate sacrifice. It also provides some justification for their adherence to a special vow to eat no meat or perhaps to prevent any possible violation of the Jewish dietary laws.

THE GOSPEL OF THE HEBREWS

The emphasis placed on the person of James, the brother of Jesus, in the *Gospel of the Hebrews* (GH) suggests that this document served the spiritual needs of the Jewish-Christian community in Egypt just as the Gospel of Luke served the gentile communities of the early Church. James is known (Acts 15:13; Galatians

1:19) to be the leader of the Jewish-Christian church in Jerusalem and as such would have been a particularly important figure to those Jewish-Christian groups who wished to continue strict adherence to Jewish practice in addition to Christian doctrine.

Here again there is a difference in the perception of Jesus' fully divine nature. In one Coptic fragment from a letter by Cyril of Jerusalem, Christ is described as a preexistent being, who made the decision to "come upon the earth to men" and is aided in doing this by the angel Michael, at God the Father's direction. Mary is also described as a "power come into the world" and thus she also has a preexistent divine nature. The effort here seems to be to divorce Jesus from his human nature, which also requires Mary, as his mother, to set aside her humanity.

Jesus' baptism, as in the *GE*, provides the moment in which the Christ is united with the Holy Spirit. It seems here that the Spirit had attempted to reside or "rest" in "all the prophets" but had only found true "rest" in Jesus. Quoting Psalm 132:14—"This is my resting place forever, here I will reside"—the *GH* is able to tie Jesus both to the theme of the hope of the people to return to Zion (Jerusalem as well as God's presence) and to the Christian idea of Messiah (the Spirit's ability to join with or merge in full with Jesus, thereby allowing his full powers to be made known).

A fragment of the Temptation narrative comparable to that in Matthew 4:8 is also contained here. In the Gospel account, it is the devil who transports Jesus to the mount of temptation. However, in the *GH*, Jesus describes, perhaps to his disciples, how his "mother, the

Holy Spirit" took him by the hair (compare Ezekiel's experience in Ezekiel 8:3) and transported him to Mt. Tabor. Naming the Holy Spirit as his mother both follows the Hebrew or Aramaic notion of the spirit or "lady wisdom" as female and also agrees with the idea of the Spirit's merging with Jesus at the time of his baptism.

THE *ACTS OF JOHN*

One final extrabiblical source for the ministry of Jesus is found in the *Acts of John* (*AJ*), a document that was banned by the Church Council of A.D. 787. Because of this, only a portion of it survives in Greek and Latin texts and in scholarly citations and commentaries. It was probably written between A.D. 180–230 in the area of northern Syria. The work as a whole deals with the ministry of John, the son of Zebedee, in Asia Minor, but the portion described below contains his testimony about Jesus.

The narrative begins with Jesus calling the disciples to his service. What makes this version unusual is Jesus' shifting appearance. The *Acts of John* provides this dialogue between James and John that demonstrates some of the prospective disciples' confusion. James asks his brother, "What does he want, this child on the shore who called us?" John is mystified because the person he sees beckoning them is a young, handsome man with a cheerful face. They bring the boat to shore thinking their long night of fishing has affected their eyes. But as they come ashore they continue to see different things. James sees a young man whose beard has just begun to grow, while John sees an old, bald-headed man with a long flowing beard.

Jesus calls Peter and Paul to give up their work as fishermen and become his apostles.

Even after they join his group of disciples, the changeable nature of Jesus' appearance continues to perplex John. He never sees Jesus shut his eyes, and at times it appears that Jesus is continually looking up toward heaven. When they recline for a meal, Jesus would regularly draw John close (see John 13:23). However, at times it would appear that Jesus' body was "smooth and soft" to the touch and at other times it felt like stone. These examples demonstrate the belief of the author of the *Acts of John* that Jesus' nature is indeed mysterious and more like God than man.

Another episode is a variation on the story of Transfiguration found in each of the Synoptic Gospels (Matthew 17:1–8; Mark 9:2–8; Luke 9:28–36). Like those accounts, the accompanying disciples are dazzled by a blinding light. However, in *AJ* John exercises the same curiosity that any person might have. He creeps up behind Jesus while he is in his divine state and is able to see Jesus standing in the light, stripped of his human garments and with a very inhuman guise. His feet are so white that the ground is lit by them. John is frightened by this transformation of his master and he cries out. His inquisitiveness will earn him no rewards. Jesus grabs hold of his beard and rebukes him, and John suffers for 30 days from the pain of that "playful tug" on his beard.

On other occasions, John is further amazed by the abilities and nature of Jesus. Miracles seem to come very easily to him. For instance, he feeds his disciples from a single loaf when they dine, a clear parallel to the "feeding of the 4,000" in Mark 8:1–8. More mysterious, however, was the nature of Jesus' physical body. Sometimes when John touched Jesus, his body was like that of other men, solid and substantial. However, there were also times when that same touch encountered nothing material, as if Jesus did not exist in the flesh. John also notes that Jesus never seems to leave behind any footprints, no matter how soft the ground was where he stepped.

Each of these tales magnifies the person of Jesus, in most instances beyond any mere human nature. It was difficult for those in the early Church to deal with the idea of Jesus being both human and divine. The stories in these Jewish-Christian gospels and in the *Acts of John* suggest that many Christians felt more comfortable with a totally divine Jesus than with a God made human.

Jesus' Trial, Death, and Resurrection

❖ ❖ ❖ ❖

BIBLICAL BACKGROUND

THE CENTRAL MYSTERY of Christianity is the death and resurrection of Jesus, believed to be the consummation of his ministry of reconciling humanity to God. There remained something of a scandal, however, in the idea of a Messiah who was put on trial by his own people and condemned to a degrading death. Retellings of that experience found new ways to affirm Jesus' dignity and innocence. Moreover, the Gospels are silent about the time between Jesus' death and resurrection. This silence gave rise to imaginative legends about activities both in the land of the living and in the abode of the dead. The Acts of the Apostles speaks of Jesus remaining with the disciples for forty days after his resurrection, but the biblical accounts of that period are rather sparse. Expansions and additions arose in an attempt to provide more windows into that formative time for the disciples—Jesus' final preparations for their work of building the kingdom of God on earth.

THE TRIAL OF JESUS

The expanded version of Jesus' trial incorporates charges and suspicions raised about Jesus during his ministry that go strangely unmentioned in the trial before Pilate as the canonical Gospels record it. There are questions about Jesus' birth raised by Jews in John's Gospel (8:39–41), and accusations are leveled against

Jesus is brought before Pilate, the Roman governor of Jerusalem, to stand trial for various accusations, such as breaking Sabbath laws.

Jesus throughout his ministry concerning the breaking of Sabbath laws and being in league with the devil (see Matthew 12:9–14, 22–32; Luke 13:10–17). In the canonical Gospels, the charges focus on Jesus as a revolutionary, a pretender to royal power and thus a threat to Rome; the *Acts of Pilate* gathers all the accusations made against Jesus by his fellow Jews throughout the Gospels. Jesus' innocence of all these charges is emphasized in this apocryphal text. The *Acts* also gives voice to the many people who were healed by Jesus. The reader of the canonical Gospels asks, "Where did all Jesus' supporters and beneficiaries go?" Now they are brought into the events of Jesus' last days as witnesses for the defense, heightening the drama of the trial. The *Acts of Pilate* helps to make the trial of Jesus a more natural outgrowth of the canonical records of his ministry, as well as to affirm Jesus' innocence, kingly status, and divinity.

As the *Acts of Pilate* opens, the chief priests and other members of the ruling council gather before Pilate. They accuse Jesus (whom they all know to have been born to Mary and Joseph, a mere carpenter) of claiming to be a king and the Son of God, profaning the Sabbath day, and seeking to overturn the Jewish law. When Pilate inquires about the precise nature of Jesus' breaking of the Sabbath laws, the priests reply that he has healed all manner of diseases when it was forbidden to heal on the Sabbath. They also claim that he healed diseases and cast out demons by means of sorcery.

Pilate sends for Jesus to be brought in "with gentleness," presuming his innocence of wrongdoing. When Pilate's messenger sees Jesus, he recognizes Jesus as the one whom the Jewish people greeted as king just days before. He therefore bows to Jesus and spreads out his cloak on the ground for Jesus to walk upon, as he had

JUDAS AND HIS WIFE

The *Acts of Pilate*, written during the fifth century A.D., contains substantially older traditions. This text has been passed down as the first half of the *Gospel of Nicodemus*.

One aspect of Jesus' passion not touched on by the *Acts of Pilate* is Judas's betrayal of his teacher. A fragment from a Coptic passion narrative implicates Judas's wife in the plan to betray Jesus. Judas was accustomed to stealing from the common purse of Jesus' disciples, taking the ill-gotten gain home to share with his wife. One day, hoping for greater financial reward, she urged Judas to betray his master to the authorities. Judas "listened to her as Adam did to Eve," and went out to make plans with the chief priests. This tradition resonates with attempts throughout the history of the synagogue and the church to explain the evils of men by pointing to the greater evils of women.

seen the crowds revere him. The priests are enraged at this display, but the messenger defends himself by explaining to Pilate how the Jewish people themselves had honored Jesus.

A second, and more impressive, token of respect comes from the most unexpected of places. Several soldiers are present in Pilate's courtroom serving as standard-bearers. These standards were the symbols of Roman rule, and generally were long poles displaying a metal cameo of the emperor's image and other symbols of Rome such as an eagle, all decorated with red drapes. As soon as Jesus walks into Pilate's judgment hall, the standards bow down to Jesus in reverence. Pilate is amazed and calls the priests' attention to this sign, but they respond that the soldiers must have lowered the poles themselves. The soldiers deny it, claiming to be pious worshipers of the Greek and Roman gods. Pilate orders the Jews to select six strong men to hold the standards upright and then has Jesus brought in again. Once more, despite the efforts of the Jews who struggle to keep the poles upright, the standards bow down to do homage before Jesus.

This supernatural sign fills Pilate with fear, and at this moment word comes to him from his wife not to have anything to do with Jesus, for he is an innocent man (see Matthew 27:19). The priests claim that this is a sure sign Jesus is a sorcerer. They resume their list of charges, claiming that Jesus was born out of wedlock, that he was the cause of the deaths of many children in Bethlehem, and that Joseph and Mary fled to Egypt to get away from the disgrace of being fornicators. Twelve Jews step forward, however, saying that they were present for the betrothal of Mary and Joseph, proving that Jesus was not born out of wedlock. Pilate takes these 12 men aside and asks why the priests are so vehement in their charges. They respond that the priests act out of jealousy, because Jesus healed on the Sabbath day. Jesus is on trial, in effect, because of his noble works.

The trial now continues much as it does in the canonical Gospels, with charges concerning the temple and blasphemy being introduced. At this, a number of witnesses for the defense arise. Nicodemus, known from the Gospel of John as a sympathizer if not a disciple of Jesus (John 3:1–15; 19:39–40), steps forward and tells Pilate that he tried to dissuade the priests from bringing Jesus to trial, saying that if Jesus' works were not from God they would amount to nothing. The priests reproach Nicodemus angrily. Another witness stands up, telling how Jesus healed him of paralysis. The priests point out that this healing happened on a Sabbath. A second witness tells how Jesus healed him from blindness as he sat beside the road to Jerusalem, and he is followed by a man who was healed from lameness and another who was cured of leprosy. Finally, the voice of the woman who was healed of a flow of blood that persisted for 12 years is heard from the distance, but the priests can only reply that they do not accept women's testimony in court. The verdict, however, must be the same. The story returns to the well-known plot of the canonical Gospels, recounting how Pilate declares Jesus' innocence but hands him over to execution all the same so as to avoid a riot.

Joseph of Arimathea and the Mystery of the Resurrection

The canonical Gospels give little indication of how the chief adversaries of Jesus reacted to the pious acts of Joseph of Arimathea and Nicodemus or, more especially, to the rumors of Jesus being raised from the dead. The second half of the *Acts of Pilate* fills in this gap for its readers. It invents a tale of mystery as the chief priests and Sanhedrin attempt to piece together what really happened to Jesus' body and, when they face the inevitable conclusion, how they are still able to reject Jesus' messiahship.

Joseph of Arimathea is known from all four canonical Gospels as the man who gave Jesus a proper burial, saving his corpse from the disgrace of being left unburied. He was, John tells us, a "disciple in secret, out of fear" of the Jewish leaders (John 19:38). In the *Acts of Pilate* his fears are substantiated. The chief priests send

Joseph of Arimathea, assisted in this artist's depiction by an angel, removed Jesus' body from the cross and gave him a proper burial.

armed guards to arrest Joseph for tending Jesus' body, and they also plan to arrest the twelve men and Nicodemus who bore witness to Jesus' good works in Pilate's courtroom. Joseph is taken late on Friday, presumably on his return from the gravesite, and kept in a "windowless room" under guard during the Sabbath. The Jewish leaders plan to meet on the first day of the week (Sunday) to determine the manner of his execution. When they return after the Sabbath they find the guards at their posts and the seal on the door intact. They do not, however, find Joseph, who has mysteriously disappeared from a windowless room. After this, they abandon their plans to arrest the other men who had spoken on Jesus' behalf.

As they are pondering what happened to Joseph, the guards posted at Jesus' tomb arrive, telling the story familiar from Matthew's Gospel—the appearance of an angel, who rolled away the stone at the mouth of the tomb, the visit of the women who followed Jesus, and the announcement that Jesus had risen. The chief priests chide the guards for not arresting the women, and offer them a large sum of money to keep quiet and spread the rumor that the disciples stole the body (as in Matthew 28:12–14). After this, however, three pious Jews (a priest, a Levite, and a rabbi) come to the Jewish leaders, saying that they saw Jesus speaking with his disciples, commissioning them to spread the gospel, and being taken up to heaven. Once again, the chief priests give out large sums of money in an attempt to seal their lips.

Nicodemus reminds the council of the ascension of Elijah into heaven and how the people diligently searched for Elijah in the mountains for three days (2 Kings 2:15–18). He suggests that they do the same for Jesus, to test the truth of the report that he was taken up into heaven. After combing the countryside, the priests' servants fail to find Jesus. They have, however, found Joseph in his hometown of Arimathea. Joseph is brought back to the chief priests, who ask pardon for their attempts to kill him. The priests ask to learn what happened to him that night in the prison. Joseph tells them that at midnight there was a flash of lightning and a shaking of the house in which he was being guarded. Someone took him by the hand and, supposing it to be a phantom, Joseph started reciting the commandments—an act that is supposed to make phantoms flee. When this figure began saying the commandments along with Joseph, he looked up and saw that it was Jesus. Jesus took Joseph from the cell to the empty tomb and, finally, to Joseph's home.

At this report, the synagogue rulers and chief priests are greatly disturbed. One of them, named Levi, remembers that Jesus' parents were pious and Torah-observant people. When Jesus was born, they brought him to the Temple to Simeon, Levi's teacher, who called the child "a light for revelation to the Gentiles and for glory to Israel" (see Luke 2:28–35). Levi also recalls that Simeon prophesied that the child would be rejected. This prompts the chief priests to send once again for the three witnesses to Jesus' ascension. Examining them separately, the priests find that their testimony agrees in every respect and so must be accepted as the truth. Annas and Caiaphas, however, speak against the possibility that this Jesus was God's anointed one. Laying aside the testimony of Joseph and the others, they point to his shameful execution on the cross. The priests together affirm the judgment pronounced in Deuteronomy 21:23: "Cursed is anyone who hangs on a tree" (a cross). They therefore go out from their meeting room and warn all Israel not to worship "created beings alongside the Creator," thus applying the prohibition of idolatry to the adoration of Jesus.

THE HARROWING OF HELL

Matthew records that, when Jesus died, not only was the sun darkened and the earth shaken but also "the tombs were opened, and many bodies of the holy ones who had fallen asleep were raised, and coming out of the tombs after Jesus' resurrection they went into the holy city (Jerusalem) and appeared to many" (Matthew 27:52–53). Here was a tantalizing and mysterious scene. Who were these people? Why would they be restored to life? Why would they not appear until after Jesus' resurrection? The Christians who shaped the stories that were later preserved in the *Gospel of Nicodemus* found here an answer to a very troubling theological question. If salvation is available only though Jesus, what happened to those who died before Jesus' ministry and crucifixion? Were the famous figures from the Old Testament accepted into heaven apart from Christ? If not, were they doomed forever to be excluded from heaven? To address these concerns, stories developed about Jesus' ministry not only to the living, but also concerning his proclamation to the dead between his crucifixion and his resurrection.

Simeon (remembered as a high priest) and his two sons are among those who return from the dead after Jesus' resurrection. The story is told by his two sons, Karinus and Leucius, who wrote down a record of all they saw while they were in the underworld. The story

JESUS AND THE RIGHTEOUS DEAD

The idea that Jesus was still actively working out the redemption of people during the three days between his crucifixion and resurrection may go all the way back to the first century. The First Letter of Peter may allude to this tradition when it speaks of the gospel "being proclaimed to the dead" (1 Peter 4:6). The apocryphal *Gospel of Peter* and *Letter of the Apostles*, both dated by the majority of scholars to the second half of the second century A.D., also speak of Jesus' visit to the righteous dead and their liberation from "the rest which is below" (Limbo) to the repose of heaven. The *Gospel of Peter* presents this powerfully. Two angels assist Jesus in rising from the stone slab and exiting his tomb. As they depart, the cross itself follows them. A voice from heaven asks, "Did you preach to those who sleep?" It is the cross that answers: "Yes." The most detailed and, in many respects, most beautiful account of this story is preserved as part two of the *Gospel of Nicodemus*, which contains two originally independent works—the *Acts of Pilate* and the *Descent into Hell*. Given their present shape during the fifth century, these texts preserve substantially older traditions. Parts of them, at least, were known to Epiphanius (late fourth century) and may have been known as early as Justin (mid-second century). Another work, the *Questions of Bartholomew* (written between the second and sixth centuries), preserves essentially the same tradition.

goes as follows: At midnight on Good Friday, Abraham points out to the other patriarchs the approach of a bright light into the dark realm of the dead. Isaiah sees it and says that this is the light coming from God of which he prophesied during his life, saying, "The people that walked in darkness have seen a great light" (Isaiah 9:1–2). John the Baptist joins the growing circle of those

Hell, presented in the Gospel of Nicodemus *as a living creature with a mouth and belly, was ultimately powerless against Jesus.*

looking toward this light and says, "This is the Lamb of God, to whom I bore witness in life, and God sent me here to prepare you as well to receive the only-begotten Son of God." John urges all to worship Jesus upon his arrival and to make use of the unique opportunity they are being given to repent of their worship of idols in life and to receive deliverance through Jesus.

At this point Adam urges his son, Seth, to tell all who are in Hades (the Greek underworld, or "Hell") about the prophecy Seth had received. When Adam was dying, he sent Seth to the angel who guarded the entrance to Eden to ask for some of the oil from the tree of mercy, so that he might anoint Adam and heal him. The angel told Seth that it was not possible for Adam to be healed now, but that in 5,500 years the Son of God would take on human form and anoint Adam himself, cleansing his descendants, healing their diseases, and pouring out the Holy Spirit upon them.

While all the dead prepare themselves to receive Jesus, Satan gravely tells Hades (Hell is here presented as a living creature with a mouth and a belly, in which the souls are trapped) about a certain Jew who is on his way. This man caused Satan great trouble while he was living, casting out Satan's minions, healing disease, and even raising the dead. Hades is afraid that their combined power will not be sufficient to hold such a man, but Satan remains sure of himself. Hades remembers that just a short time before a man named Lazarus had been pulled out of his belly, flying out like an eagle. Hades takes Lazarus to be a bad sign of what this Jesus might do if they allow him to enter the abode of the dead. He suggests that the best plan would be to keep Jesus out.

While Satan and Hades are speaking, a loud voice shouts, "Lift up your gates, O rulers, and be lifted up, O everlasting doors, and the King of Glory shall come in!" (Psalm 24:7). Hades urges Satan and all his demons to bar the doors to Hell and prevent Jesus from coming in, but at the name of Jesus the gates of Hell fly off their hinges. The angels bind Satan in chains, and Jesus orders Hades to imprison Satan until the second coming. Hades sharply rebukes Satan for orchestrating Jesus' crucifixion and death, since by dying he is now able to come down to pillage the underworld of all its souls: "All those whom you have gained for yourself by the tree of knowledge, in which Adam and Eve sinned, you have now lost through the tree of the cross."

The King of Glory then takes Adam by the hand and calls out to the rest: "All you who died through the tree which this man touched, come with me to Paradise through the tree of the cross." The patriarchs, prophets, martyrs, and all the righteous follow with joy and, upon entering heaven, find Enoch and Elijah already there, together with the thief who died with Jesus and received the promise of Paradise (Luke 23:43). The two brothers, Karinus and Leucius, are sent with the rest of the dead to be baptized in the Jordan, allowed enough time to complete their witness to Jesus' liberation of the dead, and then vanish from sight.

The story, though obviously nonhistorical, nevertheless gives expression to some basic Christian teaching. Jesus' crucifixion marked the end of Satan's power and the grave's threat. Even those ultimate enemies, death and Hell, were henceforward powerless against God's own. The story also allowed believers to affirm both that there was no salvation apart from Jesus and that the righteous people who died before Christ were not excluded from God's mercy and deliverance.

JESUS AFTER THE RESURRECTION

The Gospels and Acts record that Jesus spent forty days with his disciples after his resurrection. During this time, he convinces them of the reality of his return (Mark 16:9–14; John 20:11–29; Acts 1:3), teaches them to read the Old Testament as a prophecy of his suffering, death, and resurrection (Luke 24:25–27, 44–47), and gives them instructions concerning their future work (Matthew 28:18–20; Mark 16:15–18; Acts 1:8). A number of early Christians expanded the traditions about this period of time. Surely Jesus had more to say to his disciples before returning to heaven, leaving to them the work of establishing the church!

The *Apocryphon of James* lengthens the time that Jesus spent with his disciples after his resurrection from 40 to 550 days, during which time they discussed the interpretation of Jesus' sayings and received additional teaching. At one point, the disciples ask to be spared the assaults of Satan. Jesus answers that there is no merit for them if they obey him without enduring Satan's attacks. If they obey in the midst of sufferings, however, God will love them as he does Jesus and will make them equal to him who first bore suffering, death, and shame unjustly. "Cease being lovers of the flesh, and afraid of sufferings," counsels Jesus. Words like this were meant to encourage believers in increasingly trying times—the endurance of suffering for the sake of Jesus was not an evil to be avoided, but an opportunity to demonstrate loyalty and to endear oneself with God through obedience and constancy.

The connection between Jesus and Paul—or, more specifically, the lack of such a connection—was a problem for Paul during his own apostolic ministry and remained a matter of concern for the church thereafter. Paul was conscious of the abnormal manner of his commissioning by Jesus as an apostle. He was not a witness of Jesus' ministry and resurrection, but asserted that he had indeed met the risen Jesus in a vision and thus received his commission and qualifications (1 Corinthians 15:5–8; Galatians 1:11–16). The *Letter of the Apostles* tries to forge a closer and more direct link between Jesus and Paul. Between his resurrection and return to heaven, Jesus prophesies to his disciples that he will raise up a Jew named Paul, who will persecute the church but will be dramatically converted and, in turn, preach the gospel to the Gentiles and be handed over to martyrdom. The disciples are instructed to teach Paul what they know about the fulfillment of the Scriptures in Jesus to equip him for his apostleship. The detail that Paul learns about Jesus from the other disciples also serves to underscore the unity and agreement of the apostles. Texts like 1 Corinthians and the Letter to the Galatians could easily give the impression that Paul was at odds with the chief apostles (Peter, James, and John), but it was increasingly important for the church to assert the harmony of the apostolic witness.

THE TRIAL OF PILATE

The man who sentenced Jesus to death has had a rather ambiguous and shadowy reputation in Christian circles. On the one hand, a number of Gospels portray him as going out of his way to try to release Jesus (Matthew and John, especially). He is forced by the Jewish leaders, however, to judge against his own conscience. On the other hand, since he had rendered an unjust verdict, it did not seem fair that he should go on to retire comfortably to a villa in Sicily. It is true that God's will was accomplished through Pilate, and Jesus almost acquits Pilate of all responsibility for the verdict he gave (John 19:11). However, Pilate condemns the

Messiah to a brutal and shameful form of execution. The ambiguous attitude toward Pilate is perhaps most poignantly expressed in the *Paradosis Pilati* ("Tradition of Pilate"), known from twelfth-century manuscripts but thought to preserve a much more ancient tradition.

Pilate sends a report to Tiberius concerning the miracles that Jesus performed, the omens that accompanied Jesus' death, and Pilate's discomfort about the verdict he was forced to render in order to forestall a revolt. The darkness and earthquake experienced at the hour of Jesus' death in Judea (Matthew 27:45, 51) also affected Rome and the entire Mediterranean. When Tiberius learns that Pilate was the cause of these ill omens, he orders him arrested and brought to stand trial before the

ADDITIONAL LEGENDS ABOUT PILATE

What became of Pilate greatly occupied the imaginations of early Christians. The author of the *Letter of Pilate to Claudius* (possibly written as early as the end of the second century) recruits Pilate as a witness to the innocence of Jesus, the malicious motives of the chief priests, and the resurrection itself. Christians in the Coptic (Egyptian) church regarded Pilate as a saint, "blessed" by God for having all God's promises fulfilled in his jurisdiction. Later medieval legends expand on the story of Pilate's trial, adding details about the illness of the emperor, who is healed by the handkerchief that Veronica used to wipe the sweat and blood from the face of Jesus as he was marched to Golgotha. These legends are marked by greatly increased venom toward Pilate as well as toward the Jewish people— so much so that the Destruction of Jerusalem in A.D. 70 is attributed not to Roman suppression of a Jewish Revolt but as punishment for the execution of Jesus.

Senate in Rome. Tiberius rebukes Pilate for following the advice of the Jewish priests and mob, censuring him for not protecting a man who had done such marvelous acts as Jesus had and sending him to Rome. At the mention of the name of Jesus, the idols in the Senate chamber fall down and crumble, which causes great fear to fall upon all assembled there.

On the following day, Pilate is once more brought before the Senate and asked why he committed this injustice against Jesus. He replies that he did it because of the "seditious and lawless nature" of the Jewish people, for he feared that they would attempt an armed uprising if he did not give them their way. At this, Tiberius orders Licinius, the "chief governor of the East," to destroy the Jewish nation and scatter the Jews as slaves among the nations (a gross anachronism, as the Roman devastation of Jerusalem took place 30 years after Tiberius died and for very different reasons).

Pilate himself is sentenced to die, together with his wife Claudia Procula. As he stands at the place of his execution, he prays silently to Jesus to be forgiven for his action against him, pleading once more that he was forced into it by the "wicked Hebrews" who were planning to revolt. A voice greets him from heaven, saying that all generations of Gentiles shall call him favored since, during his administration, all the words of the prophets were fulfilled. Pilate will be called to stand as Jesus' witness on the Day of Judgment, when Jesus comes to judge the twelve tribes of Israel. Pilate is then beheaded. His wife sees an angel descend from heaven to take up his head in a shroud and, filled with joy, she dies and is buried with her husband.

Peter, the Apostle of Jesus

❖ ❖ ❖ ❖

BIBLICAL BACKGROUND

IN THE CANONICAL GOSPELS and Acts, Simon Peter stands out from the rest of Jesus' followers. Formerly a fisherman, he became one of Jesus' first four disciples. Frequently in the Gospels he opens his mouth only to show his lack of insight into Jesus' ministry, but he also is the first disciple to speak the confession that Jesus is the "Messiah, the Son of the living God" (Matthew 16:16). He is part of the inner circle of disciples—Peter, James, and John alone witness the transfiguration of Jesus (Mark 9:2–8), and they are closest to Jesus as he prays in the Garden of Gethsemane before

Just as Jesus had predicted, the apostle Peter denied knowing Jesus three times before the rooster crowed. He wept when he realized it.

his arrest (Mark 14:32–42). Jesus names Peter the "rock" (a play of words on Peter's name—the Greek word for "rock" is *petra*) on which Jesus' church will be founded.

Peter frequently failed to live up to the confidence that Jesus placed in him. Though he is the first to confess Jesus as the "Messiah," he is also the first to reveal that he does not understand Jesus' messianic ministry (Matthew 16:21–23). Although he makes the loudest promises of remaining loyal unto death at the Last Supper, he denies that he even knows Jesus three times before the next morning (Matthew 26:31–35, 69–75). Nevertheless, after his encounter with the resurrected Jesus, Peter emerges as the leader of the disciples and, as the circle grows, of the Jerusalem church during its first years. The New Testament reveals very little about his life, however, following his departure from Jerusalem in A.D. 44. A few isolated incidents, such as his confrontation with Paul at Antioch (Galatians 2:11–14), are mentioned, but other than that, Peter largely drops out of the picture.

His prominence in the Gospels, his courageous and charismatic deeds in Acts, and reports about his bravery in Rome before his martyrdom led many Christians to regard Peter as a hero. As a "pillar" among the apostles (Galatians 2:9), legends about his exploits and extrabiblical reports of his teachings circulated and gained a surprising degree of authority throughout the second and third centuries.

PETER'S VISION OF HELL

An important and influential writing ascribed to Peter was the *Apocalypse of Peter*. Christian apocalypses (after the canonical Revelation) tended to serve the purpose of moral instruction. The *Apocalypse of Peter*, however, blazes a new trail in this regard. As the disciples sit with Jesus on the Mount of Olives, they ask him about the signs of his second coming. Jesus relates his teaching on the end time much as it is found in Matthew 24, but goes much further by showing the disciples the fate of those who are condemned on the day of judgment.

On the "Day of God," all people will be gathered together before God's judgment seat. The earth will yield up the bodies buried in it, and even the animals will give back the human flesh they have devoured, so that all who have ever been alive may stand before God. As earth and heaven are dissolved in flames, the people will pass through a fiery river. Those who are righteous shall pass through unharmed and live with Christ, but the ungodly will be transported into places of endless punishment.

There follows a tour of Hell in which Peter sees groups of sinners tormented in ways that make the

THE *APOCALYPSE OF PETER*

The *Apocalypse of Peter* was composed during the first half of the second century A.D. It circulated widely and gained such popularity that it remained on the fringes of the church's "canon," or list of authoritative texts. The "Muratorian fragment," a late second-century inventory of the church's authoritative Scriptures, lists the *Apocalypse of Peter* as a disputed book, while the "Codex Claramontanus" includes it as canonical. By the early fourth century, its status as non-canonical had been established.

punishment fit the crime. Those who have slandered God are hung up by their tongues over a lake of fire. Women who made themselves beautiful for the purpose of luring men to adultery are hung up over that flaming mire by their hair, and their partners are suspended by their feet such that their heads are hidden in the boiling swamp. Murderers are tormented by ravenous worms while the victims of their violence look on and praise God for giving them justice. Similarly gruesome punishments await those who have practiced abortion or killed their newborn children, persecutors of the righteous, lying witnesses, those who horded their wealth and did not share with the needy, those who lent money and demanded interest, idolaters, apostates, those who failed to care for their parents, those who had sex before marriage, and sorcerers. This part of the vision provides a window into the ethics of the early church. It was an expression of the Christian's criticism of the practices of the society around them, as well as a vehicle for promoting certain values and behaviors within the church (for example, sharing with the poor, modesty, and sexual purity).

Those who are punished cry out to God for mercy, repenting that they did not believe the preaching about God's judgment. Despite their pain, they acknowledge God's justice in punishing them. At this point, there is some disagreement about the contents of the original *Apocalypse*. The righteous are given an opportunity to petition God for the release of whomever they desire. The sinners named by the righteous are baptized and received into Paradise. This episode appears in no manuscript of the *Apocalypse of Peter*, but the presence

of the story in the second *Sibylline Oracle*, which para-
phrases much of the *Apocalypse*, as well as a fragment
that seems to come from an earlier version of the *Apocalypse*, suggests that the episode was original. In either
case, it shows the concern of early Christians for the
problem of discovering loved ones or friends among
the damned. How can one have joy in heaven if one's
spouse or child is in torment? These documents show
how some Christians resolved the question.

The second part of the *Apocalypse of Peter* preserves
an expansion on the story of the transfiguration
(Matthew 17:1–8). Jesus took Peter, James, and John
privately up to a mountain and, while he was praying,
his appearance became as radiant as the sun. Elijah and
Moses appeared, conversing with him about his death
and resurrection, and then a cloud covered the mountain. The voice of God was heard to say, "This is my
beloved Son; listen to him." In the *Apocalypse* this

THE *ACTS OF PETER*

The principal source for extrabiblical stories about Peter
is the *Acts of Peter*, one of a number of apocryphal "Acts"
modeled after the canonical Acts of the Apostles. The *Acts
of Peter* was written in Greek well before the fourth century A.D. Clement of Alexandria (late second century) and
Origen (early third century) refer to stories found in these
Acts, leading some scholars to hold that the document
was already available by the last decades of the second
century. The section on the martyrdom of Peter also circulated independently. The *Acts of Peter* was translated into
Latin during the fourth century, and it is the Latin version
that has come down to us.

episode transpires in part as a response to the disciples' request to see the state of the righteous who have died. Elijah and Moses appear, resplendent with glory, satisfying the disciples' curiosity. Jesus then shows them the regions of heaven where the righteous dwell, and how the souls of the righteous are clothed with the garments of shining angels. Peter says here, as he does in the canonical Gospels, "Do you wish for me to make three booths here—one for you, one for Moses, and one for Elijah?" In the canonical accounts, Peter's question is passed over without an answer. Here, however, Jesus replies that Satan has veiled Peter's mind. Jesus opens the disciples' eyes to see the tabernacle made by God for Jesus and all the righteous, and the disciples rejoice. In this episode, we see how some early Christians interpreted the significance of a very strange story found in the canonical Gospels.

BLESSINGS IN DISGUISE

The New Testament is full of stories of healings, but the early church also knew of many people who were not healed of their diseases. Was God withholding his favor from these sons and daughters? Why did God not bring physical health to everyone who asked for it? A story about Peter's daughter seems to focus on this troubling question.

While Peter was healing many sick people who had been brought to him, one person asked him why, after healing so many others, he did not heal his own daughter. This girl, though a believer, lay helpless on a mat, one of her sides being completely paralyzed. Peter says that God is certainly able to heal his daughter and, to confirm the faith of those gathered around him, he bids his daughter be healed in the name of Jesus. She immediately rises up and walks across the courtyard to her father. After the people see this and rejoice, Peter bids his daughter to become crippled once more.

Peter tells the bewildered crowd that it is better for his daughter to be afflicted than well. When she was born, Peter had been told in a vision that his "daughter would harm many if she remained well." Peter had thought nothing of it, but when his daughter was a mere ten years of age, a rich man named Ptolemy saw her bathing and desired beyond measure to have her as his wife. The girl's mother refused, but Ptolemy was so stricken by her beauty that he kidnapped her, intending to fulfill his desire. A short time later, Ptolemy returned with the girl and left her, now struck with paralysis, at Peter's doorstep. Her parents found her, rejoicing that God had thus kept her from being defiled. Peter concludes her story by declaring that "God cares for his people and prepares for them what will be to their greatest advantage, even when it seems God has forsaken them."

A variant of this story is also found in some manuscripts of the *Acts of Peter* and is referred to by Augustine, a highly influential theologian and bishop of the late fourth and early fifth centuries A.D. A peasant farmer has a virgin daughter, and he asks Peter to pray for her. Peter asks God to send her what would be advantageous for her soul and, in response, the girl falls down dead. The farmer, believing this to be a curse and not a divine favor, returns to Peter begging that his daughter's life be restored. Peter complies. A few days later, however, a stranger comes through town and, pretending to be a fellow believer, lodges with the farmer. That night, he seduces the girl and the two ride off together and are never seen again.

The message of both versions is that God provides what is best for his children. Even when afflicted with sickness—or even untimely death—one can be assured that a worse ill is being avoided by God's providence and good will toward his children. Perhaps readers (ancient and modern) will not be convinced by this explanation, but it represents at least an early and serious attempt by Christians to come to terms with the problem of prayers not being answered in the ways that we would wish.

THE CONTEST BETWEEN SIMON PETER AND SIMON THE SORCERER

The canonical Acts of the Apostles introduces the figure of Simon the Sorcerer (or magician, hence Simon Magus). He enjoyed a following in Samaria but was himself converted briefly to Christianity by the preaching and wonder-working of Philip the evangelist (Acts 8:9–13). When Peter and John arrived in Samaria to confirm the work of Philip and baptize the converts with the Holy Spirit, Simon offered Peter and John money if they would give him the gift of bestowing the Holy Spirit upon whomever he touched. Peter vehemently rejected Simon's offer, rebuking him for thinking to buy the power of God with money (Acts 8:14–24). The episode ends with Simon asking Peter to pray for him, that none of the evil Peter said might befall him.

Acts leaves the reader wondering about the fate of Simon Magus, but the early church developed a number of legends about his activity after the Samarian incident. Most of these can be found in the *Acts of Peter* since, throughout his life, Simon Magus remains the nemesis of his namesake, Simon Peter. The contests between these two figures became the expression of the struggle between magic and miracle, sorcery and true religion, the religious charlatan and the devoted pastor. These stories reminded Christians of the victory of their religion over magic and also distinguished their religion as authentic in a world full of impostors and peddlers of pseudospirituality.

The stage is set in the *Acts of Peter* with a brief reference to Paul's ministry in Rome, where he is confirming the faith of many people and bringing new believers to Christ as well. Paul is instructed by a vision to go on to Spain and expand his evangelism efforts to reach the farthest known region to the west (compare Romans 15:22–24). After prayers and tearful farewells, Paul and his missionary team leave Rome for points west.

At this point, rumors are heard about a certain Simon, a great magician who has been performing wonders in the towns in Italy. Some of the Roman people invite him to come to the capital, and Simon responds, "Tomorrow at the seventh hour you will see me fly over the city gate and appear in Rome." The next day, a shining dust cloud appears on the horizon and then disappears upon reaching the city gate, at which point Simon appears in the midst of the crowd. He is hailed as a god by all witnesses and immediately sets to work undermining the faith of the new Christians. Soon, he has won over all but a few loyal church leaders, who pray to God to send deliverance lest all Paul's work in the city be undone by this charlatan.

God, however, has already called Peter to leave Judea and travel to Rome to combat the enemy. When Peter disembarks at Puteoli, a port city south of Rome, he is greeted by Ariston, a Christian leader whom God has sent from Rome to wait for Peter and lead him to the city. Ariston says that they have lost all those whom Paul entrusted to their care, but that his hopes were revived upon seeing Peter. The Christians scattered about the city hear that Peter has arrived to expose Simon Magus, and they gather together to greet Peter. Recalling his own experience of denying Jesus when tested, and the mercy he had received when he repented, Peter tells the believers that it should not come as a surprise that the devil would assault their faiths as well. He uses his own example to encourage those who have been seduced by Simon to repent and to be assured of God's mercy.

Peter's first task is to visit a certain Marcellus, who had been a Christian and a great patron to the Christian community in Rome. Whenever a believer had need, Marcellus was quick to provide assistance. Now, however, he is host to Simon Magus and has repented of wasting his money on the Christians. Peter arrives at Marcellus' door and announces himself. The gatekeeper informs him that Simon has instructed him to tell Peter, whenever he came calling, that Simon is not at home. Peter, seeing a dog tied to a fence nearby, unties him and tells him to run in among the guests and announce his arrival. When the dog speaks in a human voice, Marcellus and his guests are amazed. Marcellus rushes out to Peter and repents of having followed Simon and withholding his aid from his sisters and brothers. Marcellus recalls how Peter, too, had once lost his faith and doubted (see Matthew 14:22–33) and finds assurance that his own repentance will be accepted as well. We see here why the early church decided not to hide the faults of its first leaders—the failures of a Peter or Thomas did not discredit them, but rather helped later generations find comfort and reassurance when they, too, failed and sought restoration.

Marcellus evicts Simon from his house, denouncing him as a deceiver. Having lost face in this match, Simon must try to win it back. He therefore goes to the house where Peter is staying and challenges Peter to come out. Peter instead sends to the door a young mother with her seven-month-old son. The infant speaks with an adult voice and calls Simon an abomination before God and people. The infant further conveys to Simon a word from Jesus: "Be speechless and leave Rome until the next Sabbath." Simon is immediately struck mute, and he leaves the city to lodge in a barn for the remainder of the week.

During this respite, Peter tells the Roman church of his previous encounters with Simon, particularly how he had driven Simon out of Palestine. By means of his magic arts and hypocrisy, Simon had endeared himself to a rich woman named Eubola. When the time was right Simon used his spells to make himself and two henchmen invisible so that they could steal all the woman's gold and hide it until they could find a safe way to sell it. When Eubola discovered that she had been robbed blind, she had her own servants tortured to elicit a confession. Peter, hearing of this, prayed that the matter would become known. God revealed to him when and where Simon would try to fence the stolen property. Peter told Eubola as well as the merchant who would be approached the next day, then took four of the woman's strongest servants and hid them in the shop. The next day, Simon's henchmen arrived with some samples of the stolen property. They were taken into custody and forced under torture to reveal the place where the rest was hidden. Simon, waiting outside the city for the deal to be completed, came to the city gate to find out what was taking his partners-in-crime so long. Seeing them hauled off in bonds, he quickly surmised that the truth was out, and he fled Palestine.

The night before the Sabbath, Peter encourages and is encouraged by the believers, and early in the morning he goes to the forum. The Roman people—both the Christians and non-Christians—turn out in droves, hearing of the coming contest between two wonder-workers. Simon, again able to speak, declares the folly of thinking a crucified man to be god, and the Romans voice their approval. Peter explains that this was the working of God's plan—an awesome mystery rather than a cause for mockery. It shall be a contest of signs, however, not of speeches, that shall win the day. The prefect of Rome, named Agrippa, brings forward a slave and proposes that Simon kill him by his magic, and Peter raise him up. The crowd could decide which was the greater power. Simon whispers a spell into the slave's ear, who immediately falls down dead. At this point, a widow rushes forward to beg Peter's help. Her own son has just died. The men standing around her offer to go with her to her house and bring the corpse to Peter, if she really believes Peter can revive him.

The prefect calls Peter's attention back to the dead slave, challenging him to raise him up. Peter replies that God is not to be tempted, but rather worshiped with a sincere heart. Since, however, God is eager to turn the audience from their sins, Peter asks the Lord to revive the slave. Agrippa comes forward at Peter's invitation to take the slave's hand and, when he does, the slave revives and stands upright. The widow's son is then brought into the forum, and God raises him as well in answer to Peter's prayer. Finally, a senator's wife comes and asks the same gift for her dead son.

Peter now turns the tables on Simon. He proposes that Simon be given a chance to raise a dead person. If he cannot, Peter declares that all should reject him as the deceiver and sorcerer that he is. Simon, ready with a trick, calls for Peter's banishment from Rome if he succeeds. The people say they will go further and burn Peter if Simon can deliver. Standing at the head of the corpse, Simon makes the dead man nod his head and open his eyes. The crowds, seeing this, begin gathering wood for Peter's pyre. Peter laughs at their blindness to Simon's trickery. He says, "Let the dead man speak, rise up, untie the linen cloth from around his face and call out to his mother." The crowd offers to burn Simon if Peter can do more than his adversary, but Peter refuses, saying it would be better to allow Simon to live, so that he might himself repent, since Jesus taught against taking vengeance on one's enemies. With a word, Peter raises the dead man and urges the audience to leave behind their idolatries and worship the God who gives life. The senator's wife and her son become believers, and the church rejoices at Peter's victory over Simon.

In a desperate attempt to regain his reputation and influence in Rome, Simon announces to the people of Rome that he will fly over the city and ascend back to God in heaven. He leaps from an elevated place and begins to fly in plain view of the people. Peter, knowing that Simon's success now would undermine the faith of many, prays to Jesus that Simon would fall from the sky and be injured (but not die from the fall). Simon falls at once to the ground and breaks his leg irreparably. The people demonstrate their disgust with his tricks and leave him disgraced. He departs for Africa and dies following a surgical operation.

The story of Simon Peter and Simon Magus celebrates the victory of Christianity over magic and false gods, and the defeat of heresy and charlatanism by a representative of the apostolic faith. It also illustrates Jesus' teaching on non-retaliation.

THE MARTYRDOM OF PETER

Peter enjoyed considerable success in evangelizing at Rome in the wake of Simon's defeat. Among those whom he converts to the Christian faith are Agrippina, Nicaria, Euphemia, and Doris—four concubines of the Roman prefect Agrippa. Hearing Peter's words about the virtue of chastity, they determine not to give themselves to Agrippa anymore for the satisfying of his lusts. Agrippa is greatly disturbed by this change in their attitude and has them followed. When they are observed going by night to the house where Peter is staying, Agrippa concludes that Peter has infected them with these strange ideas. Peter also wins over Xanthippe, wife of a powerful friend of the emperor, and many others to the virtue of chastity. The Roman men, deprived of their

Peter asked to be crucifed head downward to protest the upside down views of the world.

pleasure, decide to arrest Peter and put him to death as a troublemaker. Hearing of this plan, Xanthippe rushes to warn Peter. The believers persuade Peter to leave Rome so as to preserve his life. As he is leaving the city, he has a vision of Jesus entering the city. Peter asks him, "Lord, where are you going?" Jesus replies, "I am going to Rome to be crucified." Peter realizes that Jesus is calling him to remain with the believers in Rome and accept martyrdom—the fulfillment of the word that Jesus had spoken to Peter shortly after the resurrection (see John 21:18–19).

Having returned to Rome, Peter gathers the church to strengthen them in the faith. Four guards interrupt the service, taking Peter into custody. Ignoring the pleas of the Christians, Agrippa sentences Peter to be crucified for the crime of godlessness. Peter is taken to the hill where his cross awaits, and he requests to be crucified head downward as a witness to the onlookers that the world beholds all things upside down—the good it calls bad, the ugly it calls beautiful. He addresses Jesus in prayer: "You are mother, father, brother, friend, servant, and guardian to me; you are all." Peter expires, thus fulfilling his promise to die for Jesus' sake.

The Apostle Andrew

◈ ◈ ◈ ◈

BIBLICAL BACKGROUND

THERE IS LITTLE SAID in the synoptic Gospels about the apostle Andrew. He is always overshadowed by his brother Peter and is generally relegated to a subsidiary position when Jesus speaks to the group of twelve (Mark 1:16–18). Only in the Gospel of John does Andrew gain more attention. He was the first of the apostles chosen and had previously been one of John the Baptist's disciples (John 1:35–40). Andrew brought his brother Peter to Jesus (John 1:41–42), and on at least two occasions he was singled out as the spokesman for the disciples: In one he is mentioned in the story of the feeding of the 5,000 (John 6:8–9), and in the other, Andrew brings word,

Andrew, shown here with the tool of his martyrdom, was the first apostle chosen by Jesus.

along with Philip, that Greeks wish to speak with Jesus (John 12:20–22). It may be this lack of information that led to the composition of the *Acts of Andrew* in the second century. There was a great deal of interest in the lives and deaths of each of Jesus' apostles. Their names and exploits were frequently used to promote a set of beliefs or a theological agenda, most of which were eventually declared heretical by the Church.

GNOSTIC INFLUENCES

Andrew, rather than Jesus or the authorities of the Church, serves as the source of revelation and the guide to self-realization in the *Acts of Andrew*. He takes it as his task to reveal to all who will hear him that the flesh and its needs are a prison for the soul. Only when a person sheds the needs and desires of the body and sees the "new person" within can a full understanding of the word occur. Then, at death, the freed soul can rejoin the divine, merging with the Godhead. Some of these ideas resemble aspects of Gnosticism, a version of early Christianity best known from Egypt that also emphasized the body as a prison for the soul. However, there are not enough exact parallels to suggest the *Acts of Andrew* was a product of the Gnostic community. Rather, the

THE *ACTS OF ANDREW*

The *Acts of Andrew*, written in Greek between A.D. 150–200, possibly in Alexandria, Egypt, provides a brief look at Andrew's work as an evangelist and at his martyrdom. The *Acts of Andrew* advocates achieving self-realization and a liberation from the constraints of the body. Thus the author argues for a scanty diet and Christian celibacy, perhaps based on the passage in Matthew 19:12 that says "there are eunuchs who have made themselves eunuchs for the sake of the kingdom of heaven." There is also a clear sense of dualism in this document, separating the powers of good and evil within the world, calling them the realms of light and darkness.

ideas expressed here reflect some of the concerns of a mixture of the philosophical movements of the second and third centuries A.D.

ANDREW'S CAREER AS AN EVANGELIST

The third-century *Acts of Thomas* provides one testimony to the tradition that, following Jesus' command to preach the gospel to every corner of the earth (Matthew 28:18–20; Mark 16:15), the apostles divided up the territory among themselves. Andrew's portion was Achaia, the area of Greece south of Macedonia, and most especially the Peloponnesus. In order to reach this area, with its principal city of Corinth, Andrew travels through western Anatolia, sails on the Aegean Sea, and visits the cities of Macedonia and Thessaly. The narrative of his travels to these regions contains a set pattern of events. He is successful in converting whole cities, and he establishes churches through his persuasive preaching and as a result of a series of miracles. In nearly every place, he is faced with some opposition or is forced to exorcize demons who are plaguing individuals or whole communities. No group or demonic being, however, can withstand him. Human opponents are quickly converted to Christianity, and allegiance to other gods evaporates as Andrew casts out demons, raises the dead, and heals the sick and the blind. Andrew always refuses any payment for his services. In this way, the writer differentiates the apostle from magicians and exorcists who made a living from such activity.

One story tells of Andrew's initial visit to the city of Patras (at the northern end of the Peloponnesian Peninsula). The proconsul at that time, Lesbius, plans to kill Andrew, but instead is converted when the apostle saves him from the attack of two "Ethiopians" (demons). Lesbius then becomes a follower of Andrew, and he is instructed in the power of God as he witnesses a series of miraculous events. For instance, as they walk along a beach together, Andrew and Lesbius see a corpse washed up on the shore. Andrew raises the man to life, and they hear his tale of a boatload of men who were on their way to hear Andrew speak when the devil intervened, capsizing their ship and drowning all 39 men aboard. Andrew then calls on God to allow the sea to give up the bodies of the other men. They are washed ashore, and he restores each of them to life.

These acts all parallel the activities of Jesus and the other apostles. Also like Jesus, Andrew has the power to calm a stormy sea (Mark 4:35–39) and, like Moses (Numbers 16:23–33), his word is defended by God through the occurrence of an earthquake, killing those who denounce him. In this way, the stage is set by the author for Andrew's authoritative speeches that will lay out the path to self-realization.

THE MARTYRDOM OF ANDREW

Perhaps the most important section of the *Acts of Andrew* deals with his final mission in the city of Patras and his martyrdom. As in previous episodes, Andrew has been successful in converting many people. Among them is Maximilla, the wife of the local proconsul, Aegeates. Andrew had healed her of a fatal disease and then, under his instruction, she had chosen to become celibate, no longer submitting to her husband's sexual desires. Andrew also converts Aegeates's brother Stratocles while the proconsul is out of the city. This man, already seeking a purer life as a philosopher, comes

After preaching against sins of the flesh, Andrew is sentenced to die on a cross.

to faith as a result of Andrew's timely help. A demon has been afflicting Stratocles's favorite slave. Maximilla, fearing for Stratocles's sanity as he beats himself in his grief, calls on Andrew to help. Before the assembled crowd, Andrew prays for God's assistance, using the same prayer to ridicule magicians and "the meddlesome" who have no power to command God's intervention. The demon cries out its submission to Andrew's voice and is banished from all Christian soil, while the slave comes back to himself amid general rejoicing.

Such a public display of power adds to Andrew's reputation and sets the stage for his conversation with Stratocles. Andrew now becomes the "spiritual midwife," birthing Stratocles's understanding and banishing his perplexity and his former beliefs as he had banished the demon from Stratocles's slave. Stratocles becomes Andrew's student, listening and questioning him night and day, struggling, as Andrew puts it, to be born to faith and fortified in Christ. He thereafter remains always in Andrew's company, along with Maximilla and other disciples.

This idyllic existence, however, could not last. Aegeates returns to Patras and naturally wishes for Maximilla to come and share his bed. She is adamant in her decision to remain chaste, free from "the unclean union with Aegeates." But, knowing her husband cannot be denied forever, she devises a plan to trick him. She sends her maid, Eucleia, each night into Aegeates's bed chamber and in this way his sexual needs are met. Eucleia continues this charade for eight months, but then begins to blackmail her mistress, demanding money, clothes, and jewelry. Finally, tiring of her role as Maximilla's surrogate, Eucleia tells the other servants what she has been doing. A dispute results among the servants, some remaining loyal to their mistress and some, under the guidance of the devil, condemning her. Eventually, however, Aegeates gets word of the scandal. He tortures Eucleia to get the full story and then cuts off her hands and feet, leaving her to be eaten by dogs.

Aegeates is out of his mind with rage, but he dares not abuse his wife because she comes from an important family and such a scandal would hurt his career and standing. To make matters worse, one of his slaves tells him of Stratocles's similar infatuation with the teachings of Andrew and his shameful behavior, including appearing in public without servants and doing tasks that only slaves normally perform. The slave also tells him that Andrew advocates the "senseless" idea of worshiping only one god. Aegeates, alienated from his wife and brother by this new teaching, decides to eliminate the cause of his troubles.

As they walk through the town, the slave points out Andrew and rushes up, holding him so Aegeates can question him. Despite the fact that Andrew had once saved Maximilla's life, the apostle has now become the source of great shame to the proconsul. Aegeates therefore imprisons Andrew and boasts to his wife that her "master" is now in his custody. Maximilla regularly visits Andrew in prison despite her husband's attempts to stop her. Andrew encourages her to maintain her resolve to remain "pure," refusing to have intercourse with her husband, even though Aegeates has threatened to torture Andrew if she does not return to his bed.

Convinced by Andrew's words, Maximilla once again refuses Aegeates's demands and as a result Andrew is condemned to die by crucifixion. To make his suffering last even longer, Aegeates orders that Andrew not be wounded or otherwise weakened while on the cross. Stratocles intervenes, driving away the executioners, but then he and Andrew walk together to the place of execution. Despite his brother's action, Aegeates will not show mercy and orders his executioners once again to carry out the sentence.

Even before Aegeates's men arrive, Andrew is reconciled to his own death. He reassures Stratocles and the other disciples that this is for the best. Andrew bids the executioners to carry out their work, and they tie him to the cross with ropes.

During the time he is on the cross, Andrew, smiling, addresses a huge crowd for three days and nights, saying, "Have you not heard that 'Jesus is a man who cannot be punished'?" He exhorts them to see that there is more to existence than this transitory life. But the mob does not fully understand his words and rushes to Aegeates to force him to release Andrew.

As the people approach his cross, Andrew speaks in despair that their love is still for the flesh. He asks how they can urge him to surrender once "again to what is transient." Telling Aegeates that he knows the proconsul has not truly repented his evil but is only bowing to the cry of the mob, Andrew refuses to yield to him. When Aegeates physically attempts to release Andrew from the cross, the apostle prays for the Father to take him so that his departure will be a further sign of encouragement to his followers, and immediately his spirit departs.

Maximilla takes Andrew's body down from the cross and gives it proper burial. She then spends the remainder of her life in prayer and quiet contemplation of Christ. Aegeates commits suicide in his despair and Stratocles, refusing to take any of the inheritance he would have received from his brother's estate, renounces all the evils of life, calling Jesus his true friend.

A tale such as this, paralleling as it does in many respects the passion story of Jesus, would have been used to instruct the early Christian communities. The persecution Andrew faced would have been familiar to them, and his example of welcoming death as a release from the imprisonment of the body would have encouraged them to face their own martyrdom. However, the excesses of celibacy and the passion expressed for a life "out of the world" for all Christians would have been difficult for the Church as well as civil authorities to accept. Thus the *Acts of Andrew* was declared heretical and inappropriate teaching for the majority of Christians.

John The Apostle

BIBLICAL BACKGROUND

T RADITIONALLY KNOWN as the "beloved disciple" (see John 13:23–26), John and his brother James were the sons of Zebedee and worked as fishermen on the Sea of Galilee until they were called to serve Jesus (Matthew 10:2). Perhaps because of their youth and impetuosity, they are referred to as the "Sons of Thunder" (Mark 3:17), and they were certainly among the most important of the Twelve. John is often paired with Peter in the Gospels and in Acts. He witnesses the Transfiguration (Matthew 17:1), helps Peter prepare the Passover meal that will serve as the "Last Supper" (Luke 22:8), and accompanies Jesus to Gethsemane (Matthew 26:37). His role in the

The apostle John was exiled to the island of Patmos, where he wrote the Book of Revelation.

early church seems to be as one of the pillars of the Jerusalem community, although he does travel briefly with Peter into Samaria (Acts 8:14–25). Tradition names him as the author of the Gospel of John, the 3 Epistles of John, and the Book of Revelation.

THE LIFE AND MIRACLES OF JOHN

It is most likely John's association with Patmos and the churches addressed in Revelation that is the basis for his activities in the *Acts of John*. Here he travels to many of the cities of Asia Minor, starting with Ephesus, to preach and to perform deeds that will "give glory to the Lord." His first act upon entering the city is to go to the house of a man named Lycomedes, whose wife Cleopatra has been lying paralyzed for seven days. Lycomedes is in such despair over his wife's condition that he dies of grief after showing her to John. Naturally, John is concerned since he has just come to the city and here he is with a tragedy on his hands. He prays fervently to Christ not to allow his mission to come to an end like this and then calls on Cleopatra to arise in the name of Jesus. She does, but now she must face her husband's death. John tells her to hold fast and

THE *ACTS OF JOHN*

Among the apocryphal "Acts" that circulated within the early Christian communities, the *Acts of John* seems to be one of the earliest. Based on its mention by Clement about A.D. 180, it was most likely authored in Greek (perhaps by Leucius, the reputed author of all five apocryphal *Acts*) in the latter half of the second century. Originally almost as long as the canonical book of Acts, about one third of the *Acts of John* survives in both Greek and Latin versions (which contain some different material). Like the other apocryphal *Acts*, it emphasizes refraining from sexual activity and consists of a series of episodes depicting John's work as an evangelist in Asia Minor and his ability to perform miracles in the name of Jesus.

have faith in the God who has sent him. He then tells her to call on Lycomedes to arise and "glorify the name of God." Lycomedes is immediately brought back to life, and he and Cleopatra eagerly beg John to stay with them while he is in Ephesus. In this way, John's work begins with a sign of God's power, and he has a local voice raised to support his authority to preach.

There is an assumption in many of the episodes in the *Acts of John* that the apostle must perform miracles in order to break through the stubborn unbelief he faces in Ephesus. One example of this is found in his public healing of a group of elderly women. In order to maximize the effect of this act, John stages his miracle in a theater where the women are brought on stretchers. While they await healing, John takes advantage of his "captive audience" to denounce their greed and their concern for the pleasures of this world. He warns them of the torments in the afterlife faced by those who persist in their pursuit of wealth, fine food and clothing, adulterous relationships, and power in all its forms. The mass healing is now performed, almost as an afterthought to John's powerful sermon.

Frustrated that all the miracles he has performed seem to have had only minimal effect on the people of Ephesus, John decides to confront them openly at the most sacred spot in the city, the Temple of Artemis (Paul's preaching instigated a similar confrontation with the Ephesians in Acts 19:23–40). This structure was one of the largest temple complexes in the world and was in fact considered one of the Seven Wonders of the ancient world. John purposely wears an inappropriate garment (black instead of festal white) and, standing in the temple, challenges the power of Artemis, the Greek goddess of the hunt and protectress of young women. He calls on the Ephesians to pray with all their might to Artemis to strike him dead. In this way, John directly poses the question, "Who really is God?"—a point of confrontation that has run throughout the history of Israel and the church (see Judges 6:28–32 and 1 Kings 18:17–40). If Artemis fails to kill him, John says, then he will call on God to put them all to death.

Since these people had seen John raise the dead and do many other miracles, they cry out to him to ask God not to punish them. But John knows only the destruction of Artemis's temple and cult will cause the Ephesians to be converted. So he prays to God to exorcize the corrupting "demon" (Artemis) who has deceived the people. At once the altar splits apart, and the images of the goddess fall and are shattered while much of the temple building tumbles down, crushing the priest of Artemis beneath a pillar. The frightened Ephesians wildly declare there is but "one God, the God of John!"

Demonstrations of power like this are common enough in the Old Testament. Samson, for example, had pulled down the temple of the Philistine god Dagon upon the heads of the priests and worshipers (Judges 16:23–30). The purpose of the early church, however, was not to kill their enemies, but to convert them. Therefore, John moves quickly to still the fears of the Ephesians. He knows that "conversion by fright" is not a formula for long-term devotion. John treats the new converts gently and agrees to stay in Ephesus to nurture their newfound belief until they can be "weaned" and he can travel on to Smyrna. One sign of the mercy of

God that John preaches to the Ephesians is the raising of the priest of Artemis from the dead.

Obedience to the law and the renunciation of desires continue to be John's message throughout the *Acts of John*. These themes are seen in the episode involving a young man who kills his father when the old man rebukes his son for seducing a married woman. John prevents the despondent son from continuing his murder spree against the woman, and raises his father from the dead. The son still does not understand John's message, however. Instead he castrates himself, throwing the severed flesh down at the woman's feet to show he can never again fall prey to his sexual desires. But John tells him that it is his inner thoughts and being that must be purified, not the flesh that must be punished.

Occasionally, John uses humor to get his message across. During a journey back to Ephesus, John's company stops for the night, but the apostle cannot sleep because his bed is infested with bugs. John orders them to leave his bed and cluster together quietly, bothering no one else. In the morning the group is amazed to find a great mass of bedbugs waiting patiently in a corner. When John gets up he tells the bugs they may return to their home, and he tells his friends that the obedience demonstrated by the bugs is a model for irresponsible humans who too often fail to keep God's commands.

The last extended narrative in the *Acts of John* again returns to the theme of chastity. Drusiana, one of John's most devoted followers, was well known to the Christians of Ephesus as a pious woman who had pledged to live with her husband but to refrain from sexual contact with him. Despite this fact, a young man named Calli-

Drusiana, a chaste and pious woman, had fallen dead from despair. The apostle John later brings her back to life.

machus determines to have her. When Drusiana learns about Callimachus's desire, she feels that she is somehow responsible for his sin and, in despair, she dies.

Callimachus, maddened by his desires and the urging of a demon, breaks into her tomb, intending to defile the body he could not have in life. The steward he bribes to let him into the tomb is bitten by a snake as they enter and dies, and Callimachus, who is stripping Drusiana of her burial garments, is struck down by the power of a "beautiful young man" (either an angel or Jesus—compare this with Matthew 28:2–6).

When John and Andronicus, Drusiana's husband, return to the tomb three days after her burial, they find these two men sprawled on the floor and are greeted by the angelic being. John brings Callimachus back to life in order to find out what has happened. When he has returned to himself, Callimachus confesses his terrible sins and tells them how the angel had struck him down, saying, "Callimachus, die that you may live!" He realizes that all these things were done so that he would believe in Christ and thus truly live.

John then raises Drusiana so that she may rejoice in Callimachus's conversion and she, in turn, asks that the treacherous steward, Fortunatus, be raised. This act again seems to be an effort on the part of the early church to show that Christians do not wish to take revenge on those who try to deceive or oppress them. However, when Fortunatus comes back to life he is unrepentant and flees from them. They later learn that his snakebite caused his body to swell up and he has again died. His death is therefore his own choice and John can only say of him, "Devil, you have your son."

The *Acts of John* concludes with John's death and burial. Like Paul, who approached his death as the successful end of a long race run in obedience to God's purpose for his life (2 Timothy 4:7), John also describes himself as one who has "fulfilled his charge." He has two of his followers dig a very deep trench and then stands in it, declaring his thanks to God for keeping him chaste and free of the "union with a woman." Apparently, it had been quite a struggle since John had planned to marry and God had actually struck him blind for two years to prevent this. In his final words, John calls on God to triumph over all the forces of evil and bring him and all God's children the peace that has been promised them. He then lies down in his grave and gives up his spirit. In this way, the apostle provides a model of a Christian life well-lived and prepared to welcome death when it comes.

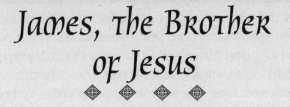

James, the Brother of Jesus

❖ ❖ ❖ ❖

BIBLICAL BACKGROUND

LEADERS IN THE EARLY CHURCH were established by their close connection with Jesus. Peter, the disciple singled out by Jesus as the "Rock," emerges as the effective leader of the church in Jerusalem for the first few years after Jesus' resurrection. Lasting leadership of the Jerusalem church, however, soon falls to James, frequently called "the Just" or "the Righteous" on account of his piety and observance of the Torah. This James was one of the brothers of Jesus (see Matthew 13:55), and kinship with Jesus became a weighty

James, the brother of Jesus, was known to be just and righteous.

claim to leadership in the Church. During the rest of the first century and into the second century, a descendant or cousin of one of Jesus' brothers oversaw the churches in Jerusalem and Judea.

James, then, emerges as the undisputed leader of the Jerusalem church in Acts 15 and 21, and is listed by

Paul as the first of the "pillars" of the church in Judea (Galatians 2:9). However, James has a very small role in the gospel story. He appeared once in the company of Mary and his other siblings early in Jesus' ministry. Jesus was teaching and beginning to be criticized by opponents as a sorcerer or madman. Jesus' family tried to interrupt his teaching to speak with him, perhaps desiring to get Jesus out of public sight in view of the mounting criticism against him and potential embarrassment to the family (Mark 3:21–35). John even went so far as to say that his brothers did not believe in him. When they urged him to go openly to Jerusalem for a festival (John 7:1–9), they even put his life at risk. How does James, then, become the leader of the church?

THE RISEN JESUS APPEARS TO JAMES

Paul attests that James saw the risen Jesus (1 Corinthians 15:3–8) and indeed that he appears to have been the special recipient of a private visit. A brief fragment from the *Gospel of the Hebrews*, quoted in the writings of Jerome (a fourth-century church leader) expands on this. According to this lost narrative, James had become a follower of Jesus at least before the entry into Jerusalem. Contrary to the impression left by the canonical Gospels, James is even present at the Last Supper, and he takes an oath at that meal that he will not eat again until he sees Jesus risen from the dead. After Jesus rises from the tomb, he appears to James, prepares a table, and sets out food. He invites James warmly, "Eat, my brother, for the Son of Man has risen from among those who sleep." James is thus portrayed as a faithful disciple whose oath reveals his confidence that his brother was who he claimed to be.

THE MARTYRDOM OF JAMES

The only other episode of James's life that became the focus of the church's attention was his exit from it. Flavius Josephus, the first-century historian of the Jewish people, includes an account of this event in his *Jewish Antiquities*. This work has a high degree of his-

VARIATIONS ON THE MARTYRDOM OF JAMES

Later Christian documents embellish this basic account considerably. *The Second Apocalypse of James*, a late third-century document, attributes the death of James to a mob action reminiscent of the stoning of Stephen. James is preaching daily in the Temple, and the leading priests, greatly offended by what he says, throw him off the pinnacle of the Temple. Finding him still living, they stone him to death as he prays to God to receive him.

The church historian Eusebius, writing in the early fourth century but drawing on traditions of Hegesippus (a second-century writer), presents another scenario. The Pharisees, concerned about the growth of Jesus' following, ask James, whom they consider to be a "just" and "righteous" man, to dissuade the people from this error. At the feast of Passover, when visits to the Temple are at their peak, they station James on the roof of the Temple so he can be heard by all. But instead of denying that Jesus is the Son of God, James proclaims him as the coming judge. Enraged, the Pharisees and scribes lament that "even the Just has gone astray" and throw James off the roof, stoning him after his fall. Like Jesus and Stephen, James prays before his death that God will forgive his attackers. This is taken by Eusebius to be a fulfillment of Isaiah 3:10, which places on the lips of the unrighteous the cry, "Let us do away with the just [James's nickname], for he is troublesome to us."

torical plausibility and is one of those rare instances where church history is addressed by a non-Christian historian.

Judea was chiefly under the jurisdiction of Roman governors from A.D. 6 to 66. The aged Porcius Festus, known for his part in the trial of Paul (Acts 25–26), died in office in A.D. 62. The new governor, Albinus, was sent from Rome, but the journey took some time. The newly appointed high priest, Ananus, saw this interim between governors as an opportunity to rid himself of the leader of the Jewish Christian community in Jerusalem. In so doing, he was carrying on the tradition of his family, for his father, Annas, and brother-in-law, Caiaphas, had been major players in orchestrating the execution of Jesus. Ananus therefore called a meeting of the Sanhedrin (the Jewish ruling body) and, arresting James and some of his companions, convicted them of violating the Law of Moses. James was executed by stoning, the traditional punishment for blasphemers and violators of the covenant.

Surprisingly, this action did not please a number of influential citizens. They protested the action to King Agrippa, who was ruler of the adjoining territory of Galilee and had been given the right by the emperor Claudius to appoint the high priests. The angered citizens also sent an embassy to meet Albinus on his way to Judea, informing him that Ananus had performed an illegal action (since capital punishment was decided by the governor, not the high priest, under Roman rule). Agrippa responded by removing Ananus from the high priesthood after he had served in that office for only three months.

Paul, Apostle to the Gentiles

❖ ❖ ❖

BIBLICAL BACKGROUND

P AUL ENTERS the history of the church as a man zealous for the Jewish law, educated as a Pharisee, whose devotion expresses itself in the persecution of the Jewish Christians (Acts 8–9; Galatians 1:13–14). He met the risen, glorified Jesus in a vision and soon became Christianity's most ardent evangelist. Paul believed that he had been commissioned by God to preach Christ to the Gentiles (non-Jews), and so he embarked on a series of missionary journeys through-

The apostle Paul wrote letters to various churches, encouraging them to live the kind of life that Jesus had preached about.

out Syria, Asia Minor, and Greece. He may even have taken the gospel as far as Spain before his death in or near A.D. 64.

Paul was remembered as a traveling founder of churches and especially as a writer of letters. Fully one-quarter of the New Testament is comprised of letters written by or attributed to Paul. Paul's endurance of hardship and opposition in the course of his missionary work also impressed itself on the church's memory. All of these facets of Paul's career became the basis for apocryphal stories about his work as well as apocryphal texts attributed to Paul's hand.

PAUL AND THECLA

The figure of Thecla does not appear in the New Testament, but she appears in the *Acts of Paul* as a devoted convert and, eventually, a preacher of the gospel herself. The story opens as Paul, fleeing from Antioch on account of hostility stirred up against him by the synagogue there (Acts 13:44–51), journeys to Iconium. Paul is traveling with Demas and Hermogenes, known from brief references in the New Testament as deserters from the faith (2 Timothy 1:15; 4:10). They are greeted by Onesiphorus (also known from 2 Timothy 1:16 as a loyal supporter of Paul) and taken into his house. There Paul preaches concerning the blessedness of abstinence from all sexual intercourse for the sake of communion with God.

Across the street from Onesiphorus lives a beautiful young woman named Thecla, who is betrothed to Thamyris. She stares out the window, looking at Paul, entranced by his teaching on virginity. No matter how loudly her mother, Theoclia, or her fiancé call to her, none can distract her from Paul's words. Thamyris, concerned not only for himself but for all men who stand to lose their wives to this foreigner's teaching, seeks to know who this man is. Demas and Hermogenes, anxious to overthrow Paul and replace him as teachers themselves, inform Thamyris that the man is Paul, who teaches that there is no resurrection except for those who remain chaste. They suggest that Thamyris accuse him before the governor as an enemy of the social order, promising to teach him about the true resurrection that already happens for the believer (they thus come to represent a heretical teaching opposed in 2 Timothy 2:18).

Thamyris hauls Paul before the governor amid shouts of angry men: "Away with the magician who subverts our women!" The governor hears the accusation and Paul's defense, and commits Paul to prison

THE ACTS OF PAUL

The principle source for early church traditions about Paul is a second-century text called the *Acts of Paul*. Written in Greek, probably in Asia Minor, this collection of "Acts" includes the story of Thecla, a convert to Christianity who came to be venerated as a saint, a rather fragmented narrative of Paul's travels, and an account of the martyrdom of Paul. The sections that purport to preserve Paul's teaching do not depart in major ways from orthodox Christianity, save for the intense promotion of celibacy as a norm for the Christian. Like the *Apocalypse of Peter*, this text was highly regarded by many in the early church as an edifying story, if not as authoritative Scripture. When the work came to be exploited by heretics, it quickly fell from favor and use among orthodox believers.

until he can look into the matter further. Thecla comes to visit Paul in prison. Bribing the guards, she is allowed to enter his cell and continues to learn from him about the good news in Christ. When Thamyris and Theoclia cannot find Thecla anywhere in the town, but discover her in the prison, they accuse Paul of having bewitched her. The governor has Paul whipped and expelled from the city, and Thecla, at her own mother's behest, is sentenced to be burned in the arena as a warning to the other women who have been persuaded by Paul. Thecla is led into the theater and bound to the stake, but is delivered untouched from the flames by God, who sends a downpour over the arena.

Thecla is released and goes to join Paul, who has been praying for her deliverance some distance from Iconium. Together they travel to Antioch where new trials await Thecla. A rich and powerful citizen of Antioch, named Alexander, takes an interest in her. Paul seeks to dissuade Alexander from his pursuit, but, when Alexander attempts to take Thecla by force, she rebukes him and humiliates him in public. Disgraced, Alexander brings her before the governor, who condemns her to be killed by the wild beasts in the arena. The women of the city cry out that the verdict was unjust, and a certain Tryphaena, a relative of the emperor, takes Thecla into her own home until the sentence is to be carried out.

When the beasts are prepared, soldiers bring Thecla to the arena and tie her to a fierce lioness. Rather than tear her to pieces, however, the lioness reclines at Thecla's feet. More beasts are let loose, but the lioness kills several before being killed herself. Thecla sees a pool of water in the arena, and takes this opportunity to baptize herself before her impending death. Several other attempts are made to kill Thecla during this occasion, but to no avail. Finally, Tryphaena faints from the spectacle. The governor and Alexander are terrified at the repercussions of having a kinswoman of the emperor die in their city, so they disband the games and release Thecla. Tryphaena recovers and entertains Thecla for several days in her house, learning about Christ and being instructed in the Scriptures.

Thecla leaves Antioch and finds Paul in Myra. She relates how God delivered her from the beasts and announces her intent to return to Iconium. Paul commissions Thecla to "teach the word of God" and, after visiting her estranged mother, she goes to Seleucia and evangelizes there for many years before her natural death.

Galatians 3:28 declares that, in Christ, there is neither Jew nor Greek, neither slave nor free, and no longer male and female. The *Acts of Paul* shows a considerable interest in the last claim. Its emphasis on self-restraint (especially from sexual relations) and its portrayal of women seeks to present a new model for male-female relationships in the early church—one not based on sexuality, which becomes a symbol for submission to the status quo. Sex (with a view to procreation) meant an affirmation of, and willingness to propagate, the social order. The rejection of sexuality gave women a hope for a greater degree of independence (if not equality) and represented a fundamental rejection and critique of the social order itself. The celibate ethic promoted by this story, then, is not merely a rejection of the flesh, but even more directly a rejection of the world.

STORIES ABOUT PAUL'S TRAVELS

A number of stories about Paul's travels follow the conclusion of the story of Thecla. Frequently, these expand on brief references that Paul makes to his experiences in his letters, but about which no real details are given (see 1 Corinthians 15:32).

Paul's authority is brought to bear through the *Acts of Paul* on new heresies that afflicted the second-century church. From the canonical letters (1 and 2 Corinthians), Corinth was known for its susceptibility to new teachings. The *Acts of Paul* invents a scenario in which the Corinthian church is beset by a group of teachers whose doctrine remarkably resembles the message of certain leading Gnostic teachers of the second century. These teachers deny the inspiration of the Hebrew prophets, teach that the God of Israel is not the highest God, and claim that the Christ did not truly become a physical, human being. The Corinthian church leaders write to Paul describing this heresy, and Paul provides a third letter to the Corinthians refuting it point-by-point. The purpose of such a story, of course, is to portray Paul—whose letters were frequently used by Gnostics to support their position—as the staunch opponent of such misinterpretations of his words. Though no longer living, Paul can nevertheless be summoned through the creation of these stories as a witness for the orthodox faith.

THE DEATH OF PAUL

As with most apocryphal Acts, this collection ends with an account of the death of the apostle. Paul is travelling from Corinth to Rome by ship and, late at night, he has a vision of Jesus walking toward him on the water. Jesus says to Paul, "I am going to be crucified anew," and instructs him to strengthen the believers in Rome. Like Peter, Paul has a premonition of his own death. This time, however, the hostility of the pagans will engulf the Christian community as a whole.

Luke and Titus, two travelling companions and coworkers of Paul well-known from the New Testament, are waiting for Paul at Rome. The three men rent a barn outside the city and begin to strengthen the believers as well as add many new converts. The emperor's cup-bearer (the title for a sort of favorite servant), Patroclus, comes to hear the famous Paul. Unable to get close to Paul because of the crowd of devotees, he climbs up to a high window and sits there. Satan, attempting to stir up trouble for the believers, pushes Patroclus from the window so that he falls and dies. When he is recognized as the emperor's servant, the believers fear reprisal while others report the incident to the emperor Nero. Paul, however, calms the assembly and, praying for the young man, restores him to life.

As Nero grieves for Patroclus, his servants announce that Patroclus is alive and standing at the door. Nero asks, "Who restored you to life?" Patroclus responds, "Christ Jesus, the king of the ages." Nero is disturbed at the young man's answer. Learning from him that Jesus is to destroy all earthly kingdoms and reign alone, Nero strikes Patroclus's face and asks, "Are you also fighting for that king?" Patroclus affirms that he is, and four of Nero's trusted courtiers also admit their allegiance to Jesus. Interpreting this as sedition, Nero orders them all to be imprisoned and tortured, and he issues a warrant for the arrest and execution of all Christians.

ADDITIONAL DOCUMENTS ABOUT PAUL

Several other traditions about Paul circulated in the early church. A series of letters appeared in the fourth century, alleging to preserve the *Correspondence of Paul and Seneca*. Seneca was a Stoic philosopher whose ethical teaching was greatly admired in the church. His moral teaching seemed almost "Christian" to many, and so a legend developed that he was in fact converted to Christianity by reading the letters of Paul and through corresponding with him in these brief letters. Seneca and Paul were in fact contemporaries (they died within two years of each other), but there is no historical indication that they met or that Seneca converted to Christianity. Rather, these apocryphal letters sought to give Seneca's ethical instruction a Christian pedigree.

Another apocryphal text attributed to Paul is the *Apocalypse of Paul*, written near A.D. 388 (the text refers to its "discovery" in this year, in an attempt to explain why no one had ever heard of it before). In 2 Corinthians 12, Paul refers to a visionary experience in which he was taken up "into the third heaven, . . . into Paradise" and shown things about which he was not permitted to speak. Naturally, readers would be curious about what Paul had seen in this otherworldly journey. The author of the *Apocalypse of Paul* supplies that information in this lengthy narrative of Paul's tour of heaven and hell. Like the *Apocalypse of Peter*, this vision of the afterlife served to reinforce the moral teaching of the Christian church by portraying vividly the consequences of virtues and vices.

Christians are burned to death without trial in such numbers that non-Christian Romans beg the emperor to stop before he destroys the strength of Rome. Nero agrees, turning his attention now to Paul, his final victim. While imprisoned, Paul preaches the gospel to two Roman officers, Longus and Cestus. Because they have not been fully convinced before Paul's death, the apostle instructs them to go to his grave early the next morning. The order for Paul's execution comes down from Nero, and Paul is beheaded. Later that same day, as Nero confers with his officers, Paul appears to the assembly and indicts Nero for his unjust slaughter of the virtuous Christians, promising great punishments for him in the future. Terrified, Nero commands that the remaining Christian prisoners should be released. The next morning, Longus and Cestus go to Paul's gravesite, where they find Titus and Luke praying. As they draw nearer, however, they also see Paul praying with them, unseen to Titus and Luke. Longus and Cestus reassure Luke and Titus that they have come not to harm Paul's friends, but rather to be baptized by them.

This account of the execution of the apostle Paul and other believers in Rome highlights the political dimension of Christianity. Religion was not strictly a private matter in the first-century world, where loyalty to the empire and to one's fellow citizens was often expressed by means of participation in emperor worship and the cults of traditional Greek or Roman gods. The declaration that a crucified Jew would return to judge the kingdoms of the world and reign as king over all could easily be understood, and punished, as treason. Nevertheless, the willingness of many believers to die for this Jesus, and the remembrance of the courage of leaders like Paul, made many pagans come to rest their hope in the kingdom of God rather than in the goddess Roma.

For Further Reference

❖ ❖ ❖ ❖

If you are interested in learning more about the books, documents, or stories mentioned here, the following books will provide additional information.

Charlesworth, J. H., *The Old Testament Pseudepigrapha*. 2 vols. New York: Doubleday, 1983 and 1985.

Elliott, J. K., *The Apocryphal New Testament*. Clarendon: Oxford University Press, 1993.

Garcia Martinez, F., *The Dead Sea Scrolls Translated*. Grand Rapids, MI: Eerdmans, 1996.

Meeks, Wayne, ed. *The HarperCollins Study Bible with the Apocryphal/Deutercanonical Books (New Revised Standard Version)*. New York: HarperCollins Publishers, 1993.

Schneemelcher, W., *New Testament Apocrypha*. Revised edition. 2 vols. Louisville, KY: Westminster/John Knox, 1992.

Whiston, W., *The Works of Josephus:* New Updated Edition. Peabody, MA: Hendrickson Publishers, 1987.

Younge, C. D., *The Works of Philo*, Revised Edition. Peabody, MA: Hendrickson Publishers, 1993.

Index

❖ ❖ ❖ ❖

Philip, 212, 220
Philippians, Book of, 53
Philo, 34, 36, 44, 57, 76, 78
Phinehas, 83
Pilate, 187, 190–192, 202–204
Plagues, 20, 43, 75
Pompey, 152
Porcius Festus, 237
Potiphar, 53, 54–56
Prophets, 200
  Balaam, 83
  Daniel, 25, 111–114
  Elijah, 24, 98–99
  Elisha, 98–99
  Ezekiel, 110–111
  Isaiah, 96, 102–105
  Jeremiah, 105–110
  Jonah, 99–101
Protevangelium of James, 159,
  160, 163, 165, 166, 167, 169,
  173
Psalm, Book of, 96, 168, 183,
  199
Pseudo-Philo, 34, 70, 76, 79, 81,
  84, 86, 87
Ptolemy, 155–158, 211
Purim, 121

Q
Questions of Bartholomew,
  197
Qumran, 31–32

R
Rachel, 61
Raguel, 126, 128, 129
Raphael, 23, 91, 92, 127, 128,
  129, 130, 131
Raphan, 97
Rebecca, 49, 50
Repentance, 16, 48, 86, 100,
  215, 217
Resurrection, 20, 21, 192–196
Reuben, 62–63, 68
Revelation, Book of, 53, 169,
  228, 229

Roman Republic, 74, 145, 189,
  204, 206, 213, 214, 218, 219,
  237, 246, 247
Ruth, 115

S
Sabbath, 80, 148, 174, 188, 189,
  192, 194
Samaria, 228
Sammael, 103
Samson, 83, 231
Samuel, 160, 162
  Book of, 34, 117, 160, 162,
  168
Sanhedrin, 192, 237
Sarah, 43–46, 126, 127, 128,
  129, 131
Satan, 16, 17, 33, 77, 103, 104,
  107, 199, 200, 201, 210, 225
Scepter, 93
Second Apocalypse of James,
  237
Seila, 86–87
Semihazah, 27, 28
Sennacherib, 124
Septuagint, 134
Seth, 18, 20, 22, 198, 199
Shalmaneser, 123, 124
Shammai, 151
Sheba, Queen of, 88, 94–95
Shechem, 66, 67, 81, 97
Shelah, 64, 65, 66
Sheol, 29
Shiloh, 81
Sibylline Oracle, 209
Simeon, 61, 62, 68, 195, 196
Simon, 65, 152
Simon Magus, 212–218
Simon Peter. *See* Peter.
Simon the Sorcerer, 212–218
Sisera, 84, 85, 132
Solomon, 19, 88–97, 122, 126,
  147
Sphandor, 93
Stephen, 237, 238
Stoics, 246

255